The
Advantages &
Disadvantages
of Thoughts

PASTOR EMERITUS JOHN M. LUCAS

Published by So It Is Written, LLC
Rochester, MI
SoItIsWritten.net

Edited by: So It Is Written – www.SoItIsWritten.net

Formatting: Ya Ya Ya Creative – YaYaYaCreative@gmail.com

ISBN: 979-8-9993606-5-6

LCCN: 2025920643

PRINTED AND BOUND IN THE UNITED STATES OF AMERICA

DEDICATION

I would like to dedicate this book to my wife, "The Praizologist," Lady LouAnne Lucas, who has stood by me for almost twelve years. She came into my life during the time I needed her most. She is a wonderful woman of God who sings praises day and night. That's why I need her in my life. I love her with all my heart.

I would also like to dedicate this book posthumously to my former wife, Lady Dorothy Lucas, who passed in May of 2012. We were married for forty-six years. She was a praying woman who would pray—believe it or not—two to three hours a day. Whenever she noticed me sitting idly, she would drop the Bible in my lap and say, "Study!" We raised three wonderful children: Steve, Marc and Monique, and neither one has ever caused me any trouble. I truly thank God for that.

I also dedicate this book to one of my greatest mentors, my former pastor, District Elder Tommy Wood, who has gone from labor to reward. I am grateful for him encouraging me when I felt that I was called into the ministry. I went to him to acknowledge my ministerial calling and get counsel about the various aspects of ministry. The first word he said to me was, *"Study."* I thought I had already studied, but I realized that I had not studied enough. He admonished me to study on three separate occasions. As I researched the Scriptures, I found out that the number three means to establish a matter (Matthew 18:16 says, *"…in the mouth of two or three witnesses every word may be established."*) As a result, I haven't stopped studying.

I must also acknowledge the late District Elder Kenneth Hoke who baptized me on May 6, 1967. He became my spiritual mentor and confidante. These spiritual giants have had a significant impact on my life as a minister and pastor.

I also dedicate this book to Bishop Ira Combs and the late Bishop James E. Kellem. These are two great men I had the pleasure of serving under during my spiritual journey. Although I'm not motivated by titles, these men saw fit to elevate me into greater positions of leadership. I am thankful for them being notable examples of godly leadership.

I want to thank my friend down in Florida, Elder Milton Andrew, who encouraged me to author this book. Authoring a book is something I never intended or wanted to do. Each time Elder Andrew and I met or talked over the phone, he always reminded me to author a book. He, along with Elder

Walter Stevenson and my wife LouAnne, all encouraged me to get started. I told Elder Andrew that he was the "hammer," and I was the "nail." Each time we talked, he hit me with the hammer to write a book. So, now he can put the hammer down! (Smile) Lastly, I want to thank one of my sons in the Gospel, Elder Walter Stevenson, Jr., for taking on the task of being my primary editor and proofreader for this project. There were many nights we sat together going over the contents of this manuscript so that this book could be a blessing to every reader.

FOREWORD

The five-fold ministry was designed by God and presented to the Church to build up the body of Christ to foster spiritual maturity. The offices included: apostles, prophets, evangelists, pastors and teachers. Bishop John M. Lucas has fulfilled at least three of these offices during his lifetime and continues to operate in evangelism and teaching. Bishop Lucas is an unsung hero as it relates to his anointing to teach the Word of God with revelation and insight. Having sat under his leadership for several years, I have gleaned from his profound teaching ministry and biblical knowledge. Having been chosen by him to proofread and edit the contents of this book, I am equally honored to be able to write this foreword.

This book is about the thoughts of God. As you read this book, remember that it is a collection of godly thoughts and biblical insight. Please take your time and peruse the written thoughts contained in this book. You will be spiritually enlightened, spiritually moved and spiritually uplifted by the points of power within these pages. The

Bible says in Romans 10:17 (KJV), *"So then, faith cometh by hearing, and hearing by the Word of God."* Undoubtably, you may read perspectives of the Scriptures that you may not be familiar with; however, these valuable insights represent the unique gifting for teaching that Bishop Lucas possesses.

As a retired pastor, Bishop Lucas still avails himself to evangelistic ministry. I encourage you to invite him to speak at your local ministry to expound on the many revelations contained in this manuscript. As you read the thoughts in this book, believe me when I tell you, his thoughts reflect God's thoughts toward us. God bless you and enjoy what God has in store for you within these pages.

–Elder Walter L. Stevenson, Jr.

TABLE OF CONTENTS

INTRODUCTION

In my early start into the ministry, I asked my late pastor and mentor (Elder Tommy Wood), "How do you know God has called you to the ministry?"

He said, "You will know the answer if you study. It comes from studying. You must study to show yourself approved."

He believed that if you fervently study, God will open your mind and give you words pertaining to yourself and give you what to say to the people. He said, "Study, study, study." Thus, I will not stop studying. I admonish this to every reader of this book who desires to have a revelatory walk with God. No one ever graduates who is a student of the Word of God. We all remain in the status of a student. When we become well-studied students, then we can teach other students. Thus, studying is an indefinite part of my life because it's how the Lord has placed His favor on my life.

The primary theme of this book is based upon the words of Jeremiah 29:11 (KJV) where the prophet Jeremiah echoes the words of God, "*I know the thoughts I think "toward" you: thoughts of peace and not of evil, to give you an expected end."* The main purpose of God's peace is to fill the emptiness of our souls that sin created when we fell from grace. Mankind is not complete until God is back in the place where He belongs. In Philippians 4:7 (KJV), the Apostle Paul writes, *"And the peace of God which passes all understanding, shall keep (guard) your hearts and minds, through Jesus Christ."* Jesus is the peace of God. Jesus came to deliver the thoughts of God with peace on earth and good will toward mankind. Jesus admonishes this in John 14:27 (KJV) where He exclaims, *"My peace I leave with you; My peace I give unto you, not as the world giveth, give I unto you."* Therefore, the question is this: What is a thought, even of peace? Peace is the fulfillment of man. It causes man to realize that God's peace is the *only* solution in life. This peace is a "thought from God" that will keep man in the times of trouble and despair, and life is full of both.

I researched the word *thought* and discovered that there are many explanations surrounding this word. One theory in psychology is that thoughts originate in the brain and are affected by what we see, touch, taste, feel and what we experience. They are called *senses*. Without the peace of God, our senses cannot be controlled and cannot determine what is good or bad. Our senses cannot give us true peace without God. We can experience all sorts of things and still hold nothing but emptiness in our souls. *Real* peace is what

God thinks *toward* us for us to become recipients of His ability to fill the emptiness.

Mankind started as a thought in the mind of God. Afterward, He put this thought of man into the dust. Within the anatomy of mankind, God made the brain. The brain (mind) was designed to be the central headquarters that controls the ability for sight, touch, taste, feeling, and every human experience. These senses affect the brain, which in turn, affect all parts of the body. The mind records these experiences so we can remember them, whether they are good or bad.

The brain has a mind that holds thoughts in our head. God fixed it so that all parts of the body will respond to our thoughts. We do nothing without thoughts, which serve as the motivation of our actions in life. There is electricity in the brain known as "neurons." These electrical signals enable the transmission of information, along with facilitating our thoughts, actions, and sensory perceptions. In fact, our brain generates about twelve to twenty-five watts of electrical power, which is enough to power a low-wattage LED light bulb. The activity of these neurons is how an MRI machine reveals activity in the brain. If there is no (neuron) activity, or if there is no electricity, the person is referred to as "brain dead" or "lights out."

God's Holy Spirit is like electricity in our brain. This means that we are *alive in Him*, even if we are physically dead in the natural sense. God's light never goes out. That's why when we hear a good word from God, it causes a "jolt" within us, which empowers our praise and rejoicing. When a person is brain dead, the mind is not functioning because no thoughts are being transmitted. The dead know nothing. We were all brain dead to God. When sin entered in, it caused the electricity and the light of God to go out. Like a dead battery, the Spirit of God quickens or jump starts our spirit with His *thoughts of peace toward* us. We are wonderfully made; yet, without His Spirit, we can become spiritually brain dead toward God.

We can "see" the brain, but we cannot see the thoughts that are in the brain. Thoughts are revealed once we do or say something. Thought is revealed in our actions. A smile or a frown, laughter or tears, various facial expressions and even non-verbal cues reveal our thoughts. Sometimes, our smile is not an indication of the way we think. There are times when even the words that come out of our mouths are not the way we truly feel. It is said that thoughts can respond to things that are affected by the past, present and future events, or simply by what someone has said or done to us. What we have touched or experienced reside in the storehouse or memory banks of our mind. The past is called *memory*. Remembering our past experiences helps us make better decisions. The present can be our conscience that is affected by memories of the past. These thoughts can and will influence our future. Sometimes, we can't go further in life due to being affected by where we have been or what we have experienced. Our future is tampered with by past experiences that can stagnate us. The future is usually an idea, plan, plot, imagination, hope or even a dream. Our dreams cannot be fulfilled without receiving other thoughts to complete the original hope or dream. But when God sends His thought, it doesn't need another thought to complete it. All it needs is an "Amen," which means, "It is so." We can put a period behind every thought of God. His Word is yes and amen. It is the alpha and omega, the beginning and the end. God's thought needs no other outside forces added to it to be complete.

God's thoughts will always keep us connected to Him to complete His divine design for our lives. His thoughts must continually come for us to constantly move us from faith to faith. Faith is simply the word or thought of God. God's thoughts always come with an *expected end*. Thoughts that God didn't send can and will be a chain reaction with a downward spiral or a negative domino effect. Thoughts we build our natural lives upon will only last for a while; but if we build our thoughts upon God's thoughts, we will build a life that's complete in Him and pleasing to Him. God's thoughts will not return to Him void. They will accomplish

God's intent, which is for man to return to His own original thought. An example of God's original thought is when God said, "*Let us make man in our image and in our likeness.*" These elements of God's thoughts cause us to be able to think. Thinking is the activity of words that causes us to perform. Nothing is done or achieved without thought.

Now, man's mind is receptive to negative and positive thoughts, or may I say, "advantaged or disadvantaged" thoughts. It is our thinking that will determine which thought will be active. For as a man "thinketh" in his heart, so is he.

This reminds me of the passage in Ephesians 4:15-16, where God, even Jesus Christ, who is the "Head" sends thoughts to all parts of the body. Christ is the head or the "brain," and we are the body. All parts will have the same "Spirit" or "head," same mind, same speech and the same judgment. The body cannot function properly without the head or without a signal from the thoughts in the head. Another word for *thought* is *cognitive thinking* or *cognition*. Cognition is a term for mental processes that take place in the brain, which includes thinking, attention, language, learning, reasoning, memory and perception. All these elements are involved in the head, the head being Jesus Christ. If any part of the body thinks it can act on its own, without the head, this is called *negative cognitive thinking*.

Such manner of thinking is an indication of disobedience. This can also be labeled as "stinking thinking."

Negative thoughts "stink" in the nostrils of God. The same is true even when we are not listening to what the "Head" is saying or when we avoid godly thoughts altogether. Negative thoughts are contrary to what God said. Doubt, rebellion, self-will, indifference, lusts and a desire to live without God, and the thoughts of God, all fall into the category of negative thoughts. It is imperative for us to know and apply the positive thoughts of God every day. We need to come to know the thoughts He is thinking toward us. So, when a negative thought tries to interfere, the positive thoughts of God will abort it. Hallelujah!

When a man's brain processes thoughts by using earthly information to learn, reason, read, think and focus, it's all based on his natural senses. It's based on his sight, taste, smell, feeling and his hearing. These humanistic elements will evolve into one's actions, beliefs, emotions, desires, and even one's will. When these things get into our will, most times, it is a done deal. As a result, we've developed a false consciousness of ourselves and our surroundings and have eliminated the consciousness of God's voice. This causes us to have earthly or worldly acceptance of what *we* think is truth. God has left the room of our mind because we have not made a place for His mind. This type of thinking is called *subjective thinking.*

Subjective thinking means thoughts that are based on or influenced by our own personal insight, feelings, taste, opinions and experiences. A subjective perspective can also be called "personal perspective" or an individual's point of view. There are many within the body of Christ who think they can move on their own spiritually. They believe they can think for themselves, without having the consciousness of Jesus Christ. However, there are thoughts of God that are called *objective thinking.* Objective thinking is not based upon one's own feelings, attitudes, senses or his own cognition. The problem is that God's objective thoughts are often blocked from getting into or replacing our subjective thinking or processes. Most times, subjective thinking is influenced by something that is materially seen or heard on the earthly level. An example of this is a part of the body of Christ, but does not think like Christ, and chooses not to think in a cognitively spiritual way. These individuals are not operating according to the thoughts of Christ, which is 'always' in truth. Rather, they choose thinking for themselves. Philippians 2:5 says, *"Let this mind be in you that was also in Christ Jesus."*

It is imperative for us to have the mind of Christ, who was obedient even unto death. As you read this book, it will increase your thought process to receive, retain and repeat the thoughts of God in word and in deed. We all need God's thoughts to be activated in our lives. Activating God's thoughts is not taking away our ability to think; rather, it is empowering our minds to think righteously. My prayer is that this book will prompt readers to evaluate their way of thinking and start living life according to the thoughts God has toward us. If we do not receive His thoughts of peace, we shall surely die incomplete or become spiritually brain dead. If we think spiritually according to God's Word, our way of thinking will not be contrary to God. Thoughts can be the continuation of life or the end of life. I pray that all who read this book will be blessed with spiritual life. God bless you and God keep you.

CHAPTER 1

WHO ARE GOD'S THOUGHTS TOWARD?

The thoughts of God are toward man (Jeremiah 29:11). However, it doesn't mean all men are going to receive them. God may think a thought toward one man while thinking a different thought toward another man. God's thoughts are directly aimed toward one person, a family, or a nation of people. God sends His thoughts in two separate ways in the sense of 1.) salvation and 2.) man's lifestyle. *"Do not eat from the tree of the knowledge of good and evil"* (Genesis 2:17) was God's instruction to Adam, the first man; however, Adam didn't take heed to the instruction. Adam's sin caused God to send His thoughts in two diverse ways.

The first thought is to cause man to return to God. This thought is for repentance because all men have sinned and fallen short of the glory of God. Romans 5:19 (KJV) says, *"For as by one man's disobedience many were made sinners, so by the obedience of one shall many be made righteous."* When man receives God's thought concerning repentance, he receives the glory of God. The glory of God is always a changing factor to man. The Hebrew word for the glory of

God is 'kavod,' which means "importance," "weight," "deference" and "heaviness." According to Strong's Concordance #3519, "Kavod" is often translated as God doing something for man or against man. Most times when *kavod* is used in Scripture, it describes the weight or heaviness of God. This heaviness and weight are explained in Psalm 8:5 when the writer reveals to us that man was made a little lower than the angels; yet we were crowned with glory and honor. This glory gave us dominion over the works of God's hands.

Again, this glory (the heaviness) is the reason God changes things. God never shows up on earth with His glory unless He wants to change things. This heaviness is the weight or the thoughts of God that keeps pressing man until He surrenders to the power of God's desires. It is how God purges (self) out of us so He can get in. The more of us that is removed, the more of Him that can reside. The more self (our ego) is removed, the more God's righteous thoughts will abide in our mind. We cannot have God and self in the same place. By man having a will, he can choose to move from under the pressure, which many have done and will continue to do; but God will continue to press. The result of this pressure or weight is to bring about reconciliation with man. The Greek word for reconciliation is 'Katallage,' which is the noun form of the verb "katallasso" (καταλλάσσω), which means "to reconcile." This word is

> God is not going to carry the lamp for us; He only provides it.

primarily used in the writings of the Apostle Paul and describe the restoration of a relationship between God and humanity through Jesus Christ. God knew man was on the wrong path, so God provided a "lamp" with a "light" for man to stay on the path. David said in Psalm 119:105, *"Thy word is a lamp unto my feet, and a light unto my path."* The greatest thought of God in the world is the lamp of God with His light. This is the same light that went out when man sinned. "Our feet" is a metaphor of our lifestyle. A lamp is designed for men to carry. God is not going to carry the lamp for us; He only provides it. If we do not carry the lamp (or thought), there will be no "light" (or life). However, if we do carry this lamp, His Word will be a light (life) unto our path (lifestyle).

God has appointed apostles, prophets, evangelists, pastors and teachers (Ephesians 4:11-12) with the voice of repentance to bring about reconciliation. In the Old Testament, it was only the prophets who could say, "Thus saith the LORD." In the Gospels, it was Jesus who said, *"I say unto you,"* along with the apostles who would echo the words and actions of Jesus Christ. The gospel of Jesus says, *"Repent, for the kingdom of heaven is at hand"* (Matthew 4:17). Jesus brought salvation or His kingdom as close as it can get, only a hand away. It was the apostles, the pastors and teachers who spoke of repentance in a way that would keep believers from returning into sin. Apostle Peter set the church in order by saying, *"Repent and be baptized, every one of you, in the name of Jesus Christ for the remission of sin, and you shall receive the gift of the Holy Ghost."* Apostle Peter operated under the influence and the utterance of the Holy Ghost. So hopefully, you can see one thought throughout the Bible concerning repentance. This thought still offers peace by the Gospel of Jesus Christ unto all men who are not saved, thereby allowing them to experience Him by coming unto His grace, or even His peace, and His rest in order to miss the eternal judgment of God (2 Peter 3:9).

> Just because we are saved doesn't mean God is through with us.

The other way God sends His thoughts is by sending thoughts to those who have repented, have experienced "His grace" and live a holy, sanctified life by His grace. Sanctification is where the real heaviness of God is. He must press us out of ourselves. Just because we are saved doesn't mean God is through with us. Salvation is only the beginning. First John 3:2 says, *"Beloved, now are we the sons of God, and it doth not yet appear what we shall be: but we know that, when he shall appear, we shall be like him; for we shall see him as he is."* We must stay in the "yet" and be pressed until the expected end. That way, His grace can be seen in our words and deeds. This "grace" is the thought that every man can experience to see the change in their lives. We cannot see grace, but we can see how it has changed us.

This thought of repentance in the Gospel was for every man who was under the law of Moses, for what the law could not do, grace did much more. Moreover, the law entered, that the offence might abound. But where sin abounded, grace did much more abound: that as sin hath reigned unto death, even so might grace reign through righteousness unto eternal life by Jesus Christ our Lord (Romans 5:20-21, KJV). *"For to be carnally minded is death; but to be spiritually minded is life and peace. Because the carnal mind is enmity against God: for it is not subject to the law of God, neither indeed can be. So then, they that are in the flesh cannot please God"* (Romans 8:6-8 KJV). When the Apostle Paul wrote these words to the church in Rome, he explained to saved individuals that we cannot prosper with two differing thoughts (spiritual thoughts and carnal thoughts). Carnal thoughts will always move to separate us from God. Carnal thoughts will invariably lead to carnal living. Carnal living will lead to death. In the Old Testament, the children of Israel could not keep the law. As a result, God told His people that they needed to repent and turn from their wicked ways, and then He would heal the land (2 Chronicles 7:14). God doesn't heal the land until He heals the man.

> Carnal thoughts will invariably lead to carnal living. Carnal living will lead to death.

Grace is primarily written in the epistles or to the New Testament Church, the people of God. In the New Testament, there are only a few verses that call the unsaved to salvation. Some may use Romans 10:9 (KJV), which says, *"If thou shalt confess with thy mouth the Lord Jesus, and shalt believe in thine heart that God hath raised him from the dead, thou shalt be saved."* Although many preachers and pastors want to ascribe this Scripture to the unsaved, I believe that this admonishment is given to them who are already saved according to Acts 2:38.

One of the key issues discussed throughout the entire Bible is repentance. Israel experienced this thought when they became disobedient to the commands of God. These thoughts toward Israel were to cause His sons to think and react like Him. Sinners cannot think like God, for spiritual thoughts are foolishness to them. First Corinthians 1:18 says, *"For the preaching of the cross is to them that perish foolishness; but unto us which are saved it is the power of God.* Romans 8:3-4 (KJV) says, *"For what the law could not do, in that it was weak through the flesh, God sending his own Son in the likeness of sinful flesh, and for sin, condemned sin in the flesh: that the righteousness of the law might be fulfilled in us, who walk not after the flesh, but after the Spirit."*

The law of Moses was weak to the flesh. The children of Israel could not fulfill the law of God; therefore, it's only by the grace of God that His commandments can be fulfilled. Grace is God doing something in us and through us, to where we cannot do on our own because of the flesh. These types of thoughts to His people, are not for salvation per se, but for sanctification. Sanctification cannot occur until one has repented and is saved. Along with

> Those who do not have the Spirit of God will miss His thoughts.

being saved, repentance is still a necessary element to stay in fellowship with God. So, regardless of being saved or unsaved, repentance is always required. God will only send spiritual thoughts toward the spiritual man to keep the spiritual man spiritual.

> Just because we are breathing doesn't mean we are saved, sanctified, or holy.

In the reality of man, he/she is a "spirit" originated in God's thoughts. To be spiritual means having a connection to God through obedience, which causes a separation from anything that is unholy. So, when God sends out a thought, the man who has the Spirit of God will hear what the Spirit is saying. Those who do not have the Spirit of God will miss His thoughts. When man sinned, he was left with a human spirit, which is called breath or vapor. That spirit is dead to God. Just because we are breathing doesn't mean we are saved, sanctified, or holy. When God's Spirit comes into our lives, His Spirit quickens (brings to life) our dead spirit.

How many of us, while in sin, have "missed" the thoughts of God? We heard them, but we rejected them. The thoughts were toward us, but we either disregarded them or avoided them. So, God's thoughts are designed to help man in the sense of how we ought to think, how we ought to talk and live. I often say that "man is only a 'thought in dust." Dust without "thought" would not be able to think the thoughts of God. Dust would be blown away; if it rains, dust will become a puddle of mud. So, man in the reality of being a "thought," is constantly thinking thoughts. It's impossible for man to stop thinking because he himself is a thought.

This may not have biblical reference, but how many of you can stop thinking? Man's mind is constantly thinking thoughts and giving out thoughts through his behavior and speech. Everything we do or say is predicated on thought. God's thoughts that He gives to us are to control the flesh (dust) that the spirit man dwells in. We know there is nothing good in the flesh (dust). Paul said it best in Romans 7:18 (KJV), which says, *"For I know that in me (that is, in my flesh,) dwelleth no good thing: for to will is present with me; but how to perform that which is good I find not."* When Jesus came, He destroyed the power of the flesh or negative thoughts where sin abides.

Any negative thought in the flesh was conquered by His death. A negative thought resides in the mind, and our flesh is the recipient of the thoughts of sin, which is called the old nature. Flesh only does what the mind says whether it be good or evil. The flesh cannot express things that are holy until it has been regenerated by the power of the Spirit. The flesh is not holy because it is subject to death. So, whenever flesh receives a thought, it will get in line and obey those thoughts. In God's perfect will, we can take our fleshly hands and lay them on the sick to be healed. We can use our fleshly feet to walk in the ways of God, even to see about those who are sick and shut in.

> God doesn't make us be holy; He equips us with holy thoughts to cause us to be holy.

Our mouths are fleshly, and yet we can use it to always bless the Lord.

Sometimes, (and life is filled with sometimes), the negative thoughts have more influence than God's positive thoughts that are toward us. We may want to go to church, but a negative thought will say, "Stay home and get some rest; watch the service on Facebook or on YouTube." The decision of any thought is what you and I will live by, so it's entirely up to us. God doesn't make us be holy; He equips us with holy thoughts to cause us to be holy. The decision to yield to God's holy thoughts is our own mental conscience and spiritual decision to make.

Man was created in the image and likeness of God. Again, man (the thought of God) was blown into formed dust and became flesh. The flesh (dust) was designed to give the man an earthly house to dwell in. More than that, God's thought was to give man a spiritual life, which would be everlasting. God is the only one with eternal life. There is only one God; He does not have a start, nor will He ever have an end. The words "everlasting" and "eternal" are interchangeable. Everlasting may include things that have a start. For example, angels have a start, but they have no end. In the beginning, God planned for Adam (mankind) to have everlasting life (spiritually and naturally); but Adam gave this up due to a negative sinful thought. He ended his spiritual and earthly life because of a "thought," which was a lie. But God had a plan to give man his spiritual life back.

God does not give us another fleshly or earthly life. Once flesh dies, it dies; but if we die with God's Spirit, we will live again spiritually. With the thought of God, regarding salvation, man can receive his everlasting life again with a fresh start and no end. This is spiritual. After his earthly life is over, he can go to heaven and live an "everlasting life" or "eternal life," which has no end. Now in the reality of what I just said, we know God is Alpha and Omega, which means "the beginning and the end, the first and the last." These activities of God are only in time. When time ends, Alpha and Omega will be complete; but God will still exist because God is eternal.

Biblically speaking, God existed before the world began. His existence predates any thought of anything He created. I have often said that God dwelled in "Genesis one and zero" before the creation began. He existed before Genesis 1:1, which says, *In the beginning God (Alpha) created the heavens and the earth.* This was the beginning of earthly time. So, the concept of time was in God's thoughts, also. This time (Omega) wouldn't have had an end if man had not sinned.

> ... thoughts are the source of communication between God and man.

One of the greatest thoughts about God is that He is sovereign. God does what He wants, when He wants, and as long as He wants. Every thought of God is productive simply because He only has to say, "Let there be" and it is so. The first thing He said was, "Let there be light," and light appeared. God didn't create anything on earth or in the sky before He turned on His light. The Hebrew word for "light" is (*owr*), which means "life." No life was created until God turned on His light (life). God is the only one who really knows the purpose of a thought. God's thoughts are the most important and most valuable things man can receive. God communicates with mankind by way of His thoughts. If we want the power of God, all we need is His "thoughts." In my eyes, my perception of thought, which may not be the way God sees it, nor you, is this:

thoughts are the source of communication between God and man. Thoughts are invisible, just as God Himself and the spiritual part of man are all invisible. When the thoughts of God are received by the spiritual man, God's thoughts are information, which can turn into revelation. Thought is how God gives man "revelation," which is information that man cannot produce on his own. The only way man would know God is by God revealing Himself, and it is by His thoughts that God speaks to us.

One of the purposes of God's thoughts was to help the spiritual man know and realize that God exists. The only voice man heard in the beginning was God's voice. He's the only God who can create and talk. In the beginning, God didn't send an angel to speak to man because He wanted direct communication with man through thought. God didn't ask any angel to approve, proofread, word/spell check, even co-sign anything concerning His creation. If we understood what happened in the beginning, then we would understand John 1:1 which says, "*In the beginning was the Word (thought), and the Word (thought) was with God, and the Word was God*" (or the "thought" was God). When man was a thought in God's mind, He was a "spiritual" man. God has always wanted to release His thoughts to man so that he can know God is sovereign, supernatural, and a supplier of all that is needed.

Some of God's thoughts haven't been revealed, even to this day. Deuteronomy 29:29 (KJV) says, *"The secret things (or thoughts) belong unto the LORD our God: but those things which are revealed belong unto us (man)."* The things that are not revealed belong to God. The thoughts that God withholds from man are God's secret things or thoughts. We must be in His secret place to receive them. That secret place is being in the Spirit or the Spirit of God dwelling in us. God always speaks Spirit to spirit. That spirit is the "man" God created. Although man may be in sin, he can yet still hear God's thoughts toward him. God only releases them as man needs them, and all man needs is a "word" from God.

God wanted all men—even the angels—to know some of what His thoughts are. Angels were to revere and keep His thoughts in heaven. Throughout Scripture, you will see where God sent an angel to speak to man about what He said and what plans He was to perform. Man was to live his life according to God's revelatory Word, will and way, which are again, God's thoughts. God only reveals His thoughts on a "need to know basis." God had the Bible written on the basis that man "needed to know." However, sixty-six books of the Bible do not reveal all of God's thoughts.

When God releases His thoughts to man, He presents Himself as the "I AM." The "I AM" is all man needs to know in knowing who God is. The "I AM" is always present. God said, *"I AM THAT I AM"* (Exodus 3:14). For all that God does, is in "that" that He is and does. In the "I AM," God can do anything. He releases His "I AM" in the "that," that He is. "That" is what He wants to do. In the Old Testament, God was many "I AM's," which is called "Jehovah." I like to say it like this: A sandwich is only known by what's in the middle of it. A piece of bread on the top and a piece of bread on the bottom doesn't make the sandwich. It is the meat in the middle that determines what type of sandwich it is. Ham in the middle makes it a ham sandwich! The same can be said regarding God. When God is in the middle of a thing, He determines what the thing is and what it shall be. Thus, God says, "I am that I AM!" God always wants to be in the center. We must have God to have anything at all! As "Jehovah," God is usually speaking from heaven, with Him being the I AM. When He desires to do something on earth, He shows up in His supernatural form and in His sovereignty.

God does things in His supernatural form to transform the processes of the thoughts of men. Then, He becomes marvelous in their sight. Whenever God showed up on earth, it was to show man His glory. The glory of God is when He is going to change things on the earth so man will not be "conformed" to his own sinful thoughts and surroundings. If man sins, it's because of the wrong thoughts he has of things and even of himself. Things were created for our existence on earth, not to be thought of as replacements of God for our pleasure. When we find the wrong pleasure in things—or even in ourselves—it is called unrighteousness. Unrighteousness is when we give what belongs to God to a thing or a person. Man fails God because he found pleasure in a forbidden tree. One of the most dangerous thoughts is to give God's glory to anything or anyone else. I always say, "Never make a god out of anything that God made." The glory belongs only to God.

If we examine the story of Israel in bondage, down in Egypt, they were there so long that they began to know only the Egyptian gods. They chose to give God's glory to the gods of the Egyptians, not realizing God is a jealous God. In Exodus 6:3, God said, *"And I appeared unto Abraham, unto Isaac, and unto Jacob, by the name of God Almighty, but by my name JEHOVAH was I not known to them."* The name, Jehovah means "I Am." This thought of "I AM THAT I AM" was only for Israel, God's people. Again, most Scripture was not written to the world, but it was written as an admonition for the deliverance of God's people. However, the Scriptures were written "for" the world to change their minds so they, too, can be recipients of the thoughts of salvation.

In Jeremiah 29:11, when God said, *"I know the thoughts that I think toward you…"* this statement was for Israel. This thought was toward God's people who were in bondage at that time. God will send a thought to those of us who are His people, kin to Him by and through Jesus Christ. He will send a thought when we are in

> We can be physically free yet bound *mentally.*

desperate times and desperate places. This thought is not for the world to hear. Galatians 5:1 says, *"Stand fast therefore in the liberty wherewith Christ hath made us free, and be not entangled again with the yoke of bondage."* We can be physically free yet bound *mentally.* Those of us who have experienced God's grace, which is God's greatest gift to the mind of man, know God is a miracle worker. God can raise the dead to let the mind of man know that He is the "resurrection and the life." We were not there when He rose from the dead; but we got the thought, for it is written "toward us" to believe.

When Jesus came to earth, He came as a man and as "I AM"—the Jehovah of God. There are three "I AM's" that Jesus declared of Himself that are the most important. The miracles of Jesus were to show man the ability of God; yet people still didn't know who He was. Jesus identified Himself with the greatest authority that His name carried. In John 14:6 (KJV), Jesus said, *"I am the way, the truth, and the life..."* The *"way"* is the way man's mind ought to think. When he thinks, he must use the *"truth"* to think. If man thinks truth, he will live the "*life*" that truth provides. Truth changes the mind. The truth will set or make us free from our own thoughts and any thought that is a "disadvantage" to our lifestyle of holiness.

When the Bible says, "*Be ye holy, for I am holy*" (1 Peter 1:16, KJV), the "I AM" must provide the "holiness." No one is holy but God. For us to be holy, we must live by God's thoughts, or the thoughts God is thinking toward us. If we don't catch His thought in our spirit, it will fly past our mind, or it will go into one ear and out of the other. When God called us out of darkness and into His marvelous light, the light was His "life." He did it by His thoughts so we can bring forth His praise. Owr, the Hebrew word for "light" is the same light that Elohim, who is God, called forth in the beginning of creation. This light (owr) is the same word as "life." While we were in darkness, our minds were blind to the light or life of God. God's light can come into darkness, but darkness cannot come into His light or His life. There is no darkness in Him at all. The "light" or "life" of God is to give us cognitive knowledge of a lifestyle that His light and His life provide.

Once again, the knowledge must be received, retained and repeated in our minds until it transforms into word and/or deed. Our flesh is not holy; it is used to present what is holy. We should not just be hearers of God's knowledge, but doers of His knowledge. I am sure most of us know that knowledge is the key to life. We won't just grow old, but we'll grow up with the understanding of God. Proverbs 1:2-5 & 7 (KJV) says, *"To know wisdom and instruction; to perceive the words of understanding; to receive the instruction of wisdom, justice, and judgment, and equity; to give subtilty to the simple, to the young man knowledge and discretion. A wise man will hear, and will increase learning; and a man of understanding shall attain unto wise counsels: The fear of the LORD is the "beginning" of knowledge: but fools despise wisdom and instruction."* The first chapter of Proverbs is written by Solomon, son of David, king of Israel. The first few verses give us an example of what is called "true cognitive" or "cognition knowledge."

The young, the old, and all that's in between need to adapt to these wise sayings of Solomon. Solomon received his wisdom from God's "thoughts." We are living in a world where man has become "wise in his own eyes," but true wisdom is not to walk by sight, but by faith. Faith is the wisdom of God. Wisdom (which is God) is the principal of life; so, let's get wisdom (or let's get God). In all our getting, let's get understanding (or let's get God's mind). His understanding is only provided by the thoughts God is thinking toward us.

In summary, man is only a "thought" in formed dust, or what is called "flesh." The difficult part of God giving man His thoughts is that man could not complete God's thoughts in the flesh without God thus, giving man his expected end required grace. Grace is God doing "that" which is impossible for us to do ourselves, including living holy. God came as His own thought (in the person of Jesus Christ) to change the mind of mankind and his thoughts. Colossians 3:1-2 says, *"If ye then be risen with Christ, seek (investigate, prove) those things which are above, where Christ sitteth on the right hand of God. Set your affection on things above, not on things on the earth."* We cannot prove or investigate anything in heaven without being resurrected by God's Spirit. His Spirit gives us access to heavenly things. If we perceive with our natural eyes or thoughts, we will see the Son of man as a literal person, sitting at the right hand of the Father. You will see "two Gods"—the Father and the Son. God doesn't have a "junior God." There will never be two Gods in heaven. We will miss who the right hand really is. The right hand of God is His Word, which is Jesus Christ. Jesus is called a man, as a metaphoric manifestation of God's Word. The right hand of God is the hand of distribution. We get nothing from God unless His right hand, who is Jesus (the Word of God), gives it to us. This is a mental and spiritual picture of the three in heaven who are "one."

Colossians 3:2 says, *"Set your affection..."* (or fix your mind). This lets us know we can control our minds. We can fix our minds on things above, not on things on the earth. That's when we will understand how the Father, the Word, which is the Son, and Holy Spirit are one.

Fixing our minds on things above allows us to receive the thoughts that God is thinking toward us. Please remember that God's thoughts are always toward you. They are of peace and not of evil, to give you His expected end.

God bless you.

CHAPTER 2

THE POWER OF THOUGHT

I sit in a big chair during my quiet time with God. I found out that the best time to sit there is in the mornings. In Psalm 63:1 (KJV), David wrote, "O God, *thou art my God; early will I seek thee...*" What David was seeking was more thoughts of God. To me, David was saying that the early hour is the best time to seek God. Receiving early thoughts from God is an excellent way to start the day. I sit in my big chair early, while everyone is asleep or at work. Since I've retired, I sit there, meditating on the grace and mercies of God. That's the place where God and I meet. I call it The Secret Place. That's where God gives me some "sacred thoughts." Even when God gives us Scripture(s) to read, it's God's way of giving us His thoughts. That's where I learned about the power of thought.

The mind is the only part of man that has thoughts. One of the greatest powers of thought is that it allows us to think of things from the past, things in our present, and things in our future. Thoughts can be considered a "time machine." Thoughts can travel to places we have left or been to. They can travel to where we are in the moment and where we want to go in the future. It only takes a nanosecond to go where thoughts will take us. Now, as powerful as thoughts are, we can change the direction of thoughts. Sometimes, we think more about the future when we should focus on our present. We cannot change history; but the thoughts of yesterday can and will affect our present. The thoughts in our mind can travel forward and backward. Our thoughts can determine what we desire right now. Thoughts also allow us to think of heavenly or spiritual things.

Our thoughts are so powerful that they can go to heaven before we get there. Thoughts can reach the throne of grace, while our feet are still on earth. Thoughts allow our bodies to be in one place and our minds in another place. They allow us to have visions, dreams, and even daydreams. Just ask the Apostle Paul, who was lifted through or by a spiritual thought into the third heaven to meet and greet God, who created thoughts. Paul may not have seen God, but he heard Him talk. His eyes saw what heaven looks like, and God instructed him not to repeat all that he had seen.

Once our eyes see things, it registers in our minds as a mental picture or thought. We have not yet experienced what Apostle Paul has seen, but we will. God fixed it for us to read (as a thought) about what heaven looks like in the Revelation so we could have a mental picture of heaven in our memory banks. That way, when we encounter trouble in this life, we can draw from our memory banks, knowing where we are going and that trouble won't last always. We will get through every trial or tribulation. We can see our future just by thinking about it.

Thoughts can promote both positive and negative feelings. Thoughts can cause anxiety, stress, disappointment, and discouragement. On the flip side, they can also cause joy, happiness and peace. God's thoughts are so powerful that they called us out of darkness into His marvelous light. The Greek word for "call" is '*phoneo*,' which means, "a personal call." It's only for the one who "answers" the call. Back in the day, there was something called a "personal call" or a "long-distance call." It was more expensive than a regular or local call. God made a personal, long-distance call that cost the life of Jesus Christ. It was free for us; however, it cost the caller a lot. Collectively, we are the whole body of Christ; but God called us individually. When any man answers the call, God gives them enlightenment. The prefix "en" means "within." We must be "within" or totally engulfed by the light (or life). When we are within it, our thoughts change to a better understanding of His thoughts. It will guide us through the dark places of life.

We can allow His thoughts, which has become our life, to shine so that men might see our good works and glorify the

Father, which is in heaven. Naturally, a thought is an idea, plan, plot, or imagination. Sometimes, a thought will suddenly appear as we often say, from nowhere. Most times, what we see, hear, touch or experience can trigger a thought. Our senses trigger thoughts or promote thinking. In this thinking, there must be some thoughts already in the mind to evaluate or process incoming thoughts. If there is no correct knowledge (which is God's truth) already present, we will assume. Most times, an assumption is not the truth or proof. The truth of God is not an assumption or an opinion. God never gives us His assumptions or opinions. He says what He means and means what He says.

Truth is not an opinion, an idea nor an imagination. It is the absolute solution for every incoming thought. We will never hear God say, "My opinion is…" God's thoughts are not what He thinks will happen; His thoughts will *make* it happen. The truth of God is known as His "Alpha and Omega." He proved Himself in between both. The reality of the truth of God is that God can tell us something way before it happens. Satan must wait until it is spoken or until it happens before he moves to interrupt things. Yet, when we see what God said come to pass, we know that God is truthful and faithful to His Word.

Second Corinthians 10:5 says, "*Casting down imaginations and every high thing that exalteth itself against the knowledge of God"* (or God's truth). These imaginations can be any plot of Satan or even our own ego. God will not come and "get" these carnal thoughts from our mind. We must bring our thoughts under the obedience of Christ. Again, it's always good to bring our thoughts into alignment with God's thoughts because every thought may not be correct knowledge. We should never obey every thought because our mind is susceptible to all kinds of thoughts, both good and evil. We should put on the mind of Christ.

When God speaks peace, it will cause our mind to be at peace, knowing that God will fight our battles. God's peace will win the battle for us. God is the truth, the absolute reality of life. There is no problem on earth that His truth cannot solve or bring peace to. God's Word is truth. The Hebrew word for truth is '*emet*.' Emet is significant because it contains the first, middle, and last letters of the Hebrew alphabet, signifying that truth encompasses all things and endures from beginning to end. This is because God's Word is truth. God's consistent thoughts are also truth.

How is it that God chose forty to forty-five men or so to write the Bible with a consistency of the same thought of Jesus Christ, before and after He came? It's difficult to get two men or two women to agree on anything. I Timothy 3:16 says, *"And without controversy great is the mystery of godliness: God was manifest in the flesh, justified in the Spirit, seen of angels, preached unto the Gentiles, believed on in the world, received up into glory."* The truth is in the eye or thoughts of the beholder. Our eyes must be enlightened with the inspiration of God.

In the Old Testament, the one consistent thought was all about Jesus Christ. He is the Logos or thought of God concealed. In the New Testament, Jesus Christ is God's thought revealed. He is the *'Rhema'* of God's Word, which means "a word that has already been spoken or written and received." Jesus Christ is the *'epos,'* meaning "poetic expression" or the "articulated expression" of God in us and through us. Epos is the Word of God activated in us to do what is righteous. The reality of the epos is that it is the "final true expression of the Logos" or the thought of God, seen in word or deed. We are to be the living epistles, read and known of men. All three—the Logos, Rhema and Epos are combined into one complete thought. So, God's Word cannot and will not return unto Him void.

The thought of God that created mankind was so powerful that it caused man to become a living soul. In the Hebrew, one of the words for soul is *'nephesh,'* which means "breath" or a "living being." It is said that the soul is made up of two parts: spirit and flesh. The flesh pertains to dust, and the spirit pertains to the spirit of the man, being the thought of God. It is up to the soul whether the man will live by the flesh or live by the spirit. The spirit of man will always represent the thought of God, or it will represent man being in God's image and likeness. If man's soul would've maintained who he originally was—the thought of God—he would've continued to live an everlasting life. That was the purpose of "the tree of life"—the content of God's vision.

However, since man's soul chose to live by the flesh (dust), he must surely die. This is why the last words spoken over man after death is… "ashes to ashes, dust to dust." I can't find anywhere in the beginning where God ever told the man, "You will live forever." That was because God didn't have to say it; "living" was already designed into the man. It was through man's disobedience that living was interrupted. Just maybe, the man didn't fully understand what "everlasting life" was. God told the man the thought that would keep him alive forever. Satan took this thought of God and twisted it so that man "thought" what God said was a disadvantage to him. Satan told man that, "*God knows that in the day that you eat of the tree – you shall be like God knowing good and evil.*" This statement from the devil was a lie. God had already revealed to man the commandment "*for in the day that you eat of the tree of the knowledge of the good and evil, you will surely die.*" This thought from God also served as an advantage to man to maintain life. Yet, man rejected it and death manifested.

This thought of God was a warning from God. Seems to me that Satan also heard this warning. Satan had to wait until the thought was released. He then changed the context of God's thought in his discourse with Eve. Then, a battle of thoughts took place in her mind. God's thought versus the thought of the enemy. However, we have the power to cast those negative thoughts down according to 2 Corinthians 10:5. Sometimes, we want God to change our mind, when He has already given us the power to do so ourselves. We are not waiting on God; God is waiting on us. It's up to us to change our mind in accordance with the thoughts God is thinking toward us, even His written Word. Satan came with a powerful thought against what God said. Satan also must have heard the first thought that God gave man that was in the form of a command—for man to be fruitful, and multiply, and replenish the earth, and subdue it with his own kind, being in the image and likeness of God (Genesis 1:28).

Initially, Adam didn't have a helpmeet to multiply and replenish the earth with one of his own kind, so God thought in Genesis 2:18 that, *"It's not good for man to be alone. I will give him an help meet."*

Therefore, He created Eve, the first woman. By God releasing that thought, Satan didn't go after Adam; Satan went after God's plan. The woman was God's plan to help man in multiplying and replenishing the earth. Satan went after the woman to make sure no man would be born in the image and likeness of God. All men would be born as sinners, with thoughts contrary to the thoughts of God and thoughts about God.

All nations came "out" of Adam with a negative thought called sin; but now, with the positive thought of the gospel, all men must go in and through Jesus Christ to be born again. *"If any man be in Christ, he is a new creation. Old things are passed away; behold, all things are become new"* (2 Corinthians 5:17). Now, the question becomes, "Where did the negative thought originate from?" It originated in heaven. One would think heaven has no negative thoughts since it's eternal. I believe angels have thoughts, too. Lucifer was a perfect angel; however, he had a negative thought called pride. Any time we want what exclusively belongs to God, it's called unrighteousness, which is the source of pride. Lucifer wanted the glory that belonged only to God. *"How art thou fallen from heaven, O Lucifer, son of the morning! How art thou cut down to the ground, which didst weaken the nations! For thou hast said in thine heart, I will ascend into heaven, I will exalt my throne above the stars of God: I will sit also upon the mount of the congregation, in the sides of the north: I will ascend above the heights of the clouds; I will be like The Most High"* (Isaiah 14:12-14, KJV).

Lucifer didn't want to get rid of God; he wanted to be God's "God." This was the first negative thought. God heard Lucifer's thought that was in his heart. And as Lucifer thought in his heart, he was. He was a liar! Lucifer became Satan, who is an eternal liar, and he will never change. Satan brought that same thought or lie to earth to weaken all nations. Satan came to kill, steal, and destroy mankind with a negative (disadvantaged) thought against God.

A lie is always a thought in our hearts before it comes out of our mouths, for out of the abundance of the heart, the mouth speaketh. Lying is a matter of the heart. It resides in our hearts most times without us knowing. However, it will manifest itself in a *New York second*. A lie can sometimes sound better than the truth. A lie can be a strong thought—even a stronghold. However, it is up to us to know the truth that sets us free from a lie. The thoughts of God in His Word helps us to differentiate between the truth and the lie.

We have given the "man" a new characteristic called "humanity." Nowhere in the Bible did God ever call man "*human*." Human is a two-part word that is made up of "hu" or "hue," and "man." Hue is the color of dirt or dust that the thought of man dwells in. This is why we have so many colors of humans. God only sends His thoughts to the "man" (or spirit), not to the hue or dirt. The

> If he could destroy man's flesh, he could destroy man's soul and his spirit by the thoughts of disobedience and rebellion against God.

thought that Satan brought to humanity was to destroy his spirit. Satan did this through man's flesh, which was as weak as the dust it was made from. If he could destroy man's flesh, he could destroy man's soul and his spirit by the thoughts of disobedience and rebellion against God.

So, man, being a living soul, satisfied the "hue" and not the spirit, to which he was. This is why unsaved human beings are known as "lost souls." They are not born of the Spirit of God. Now, man only has a consciousness of *his* surroundings and consciousness of *himself*—and not of God. Jesus came to save the man's soul, not the "hue" or man's flesh. If Satan could get the hue or flesh to eat of the forbidden tree, he could kill, steal and destroy the man's spirit. Soon after, the hue or flesh would also die. Satan wants man to have a dead spirit, much like his own spirit. Satan said, "You won't surely die." But God said, "You *will* surely die." I have learned to never put a *won't* on God's *will*!

Now man is a trichotomy or a three-dimensional being. The man is a spiritual thought who was fashioned in dirt or dust and became a living soul. Man died trying to satisfy the dirt (flesh) rather than the image and likeness of God. *If the man in the hue or flesh doesn't maintain the thoughts of God, he would lose the reflection or glory of God.* God's Word would feed the man, and in return, the reflection or glory of God would be displayed in the hue or flesh. The thoughts that control the mind control the flesh. When man allowed the negative (disadvantaged) thought to enter his mind, the flesh began to decompose. This negative thought destroyed man's soul where the heart, mind, will, emotions and desires all abide. This negative thought entered the deepest portion of man, which is in his heart.

The heart is where God wants to abide. According to the Hebrew definition, the heart is the center of man, and God always desires to be in the center. The Bible clarifies this, right in the center of the Bible. Psalm 118:8-9 (KJV) says, *"It is better to trust in the LORD than to put confidence in man. It is better to trust in the LORD than to put confidence in princes"* (government). The heart of man is the place where God wants His desires and His thoughts to reside. Psalm 37:4 says that God will give you the desires of your heart (paraphrased). If God is in our hearts, our desires will be His desires. If God is not in our hearts, He is not obligated to fulfill the desires. As a man thinks in his heart, so is he. Man doesn't know what is in his heart because his heart is buried in dirt or the dust. Only God knows what's in man's heart. On the day of Pentecost, the Bible says that the people were pricked in their "hearts." When we came to God, all our hearts were buried in dirt. God is the only one who can search the heart and try the reins of the heart. God will send His Word as a bulldozer to remove the dirt!

There is another side to evil that's called rebellion. The Hebrew word for rebellion is '*mārâ*' (maw-raw). It means "to be contentious, to be rebellious, to be refractory, to be disobedient towards, to be rebellious against." Rebellion is knowing what to do yet refusing to do it. On the other hand, we can be ignorant or unlearned concerning the standards of God. The Apostle Paul (before his conversion) was ignorant concerning the Church, and his conscience didn't bother him concerning the Church. When God met Paul (who was Saul at that time) on the road to Damascus, He brought his ignorance to a screeching halt. Whether we know or don't know, it will not stop God's judgment. I believe every man will hear the standards of God before He returns in the clouds in the sky.

If I were God, I would have never given man a will. The reason I say this is because the will of man is the creative expression of everything that's in his soul. When we promise God, "I will," it involves our mind, heart, desires, emotions, and strength. Our will is the greatest result of our thoughts. It causes action, or the "volition" to do—whether it is right or wrong. God has said, "*My thoughts are not your thoughts, and My will (ways) is not your will*" (paraphrased) (Isaiah 55:8, KJV). We will be destroyed by our thoughts if our thoughts are not God's thoughts. We will have an unexpected end called "judgment." God said, "*I know the thoughts that I think toward you...*" The operative word in this verse is "toward," meaning you can receive it or deny it. It's like when someone throws a ball toward you; you can catch it or let it fly over your head. God's thoughts are of peace and not of evil, or of judgment. We have the same mind after salvation that we had when we were in sin. However, now, our mind must be renewed by cognition of the Word of God. Then, our thoughts will be His thoughts, and our ways will be His ways.

Most times, as I often say, "We learn by burn." Some of us learn lessons in hindsight to what God has said and done, and that's a burn we will not forget. The song says, "Jesus, I'll never forget…" Sometimes, our thoughts of the past are only about how God brought us out; however, we should also remember how we got into the trouble so that we won't repeat the same mistakes again. Then, we will learn to apply more of His thoughts in the future.

In Philippians 3:14, Apostle Paul said, "*I press toward the mark for the prize of the high calling of God in Christ Jesus.*" If we don't hit the mark, we won't get the prize. We cannot get the prize if we are not in Christ. The press is like a mode of transportation. It is fueled by faith in action that steers us toward the mark. Our elders would tell us, "Press your way." I believe what they were trying to say to us was to move your faith toward God, and God will move His thoughts toward you. In life, we only learn two basic things:

what to do and what *not* to do. The key to this is *wisdom*. When we come to a point in life that we can't differentiate which one to choose, we need wisdom or a thought from God. The Hebrew word for wisdom is '*hakham,*' which means "to be wise and skillful" or "to be more articulate in the way we think." Many of our sins happen because we didn't have the wisdom of God; or we *have* the wisdom of God and simply didn't use it.

Wisdom is primarily a revelatory thought of God. God's revelation is the revealing of God's thoughts toward us. Again, we must receive it, retain it, and repeat it, in word and deed. This is a terrific way to consistently perform what to do and what not to do. The wise man Solomon said in Proverbs 4:7 (KJV), "*Wisdom is the principal thing; therefore, get wisdom: and with all thy getting get understanding.*" Allow me to paraphrase this verse: God is the principal thing, so get God; and in all thy getting, get God's mind or His understanding. Without wisdom, man will think he knows his own ways, and he will think highly of himself, which is called pride. Proverbs 16:18 (KJV) says, "*Pride goeth before destruction, and a haughty spirit before a fall.*" Pride is an incompetent spirit that fails to receive God's thoughts that are toward mankind. When man thinks he knows it all, he really doesn't know his next step. Man doesn't have the capacity or ability to know everything about life. Pride sets in and pride has a disadvantaged end.

Man began to virtually live with no conscience of himself or his surroundings. So, God sent a thought to a man named Noah, whose name means *"rest."* The flood was God's judgment call because man's thoughts and senses were out of control. Genesis 6:5 (KJV) was much like the times we live in today called "perilous times." It says, *"And God saw that the wickedness of man was great in the earth, and that every imagination of the thoughts of his heart was only evil continually."* But God still had a thought toward Noah. Noah found grace in the sight of God. Violence and riotous living took place at that time, and God decided to remove all men from the face of the earth. God had not been this upset since the beginning of time when He put Adam and Eve out of the garden. [*When man ate of the tree in the garden, in disobedience, he tapped into the righteous judgement of God. This was something that had never been introduced to mankind. His disobedience brought forth something that was never intended for him. God never wanted mankind to experience His righteous judgement.*] God is that upset with man today. We who are in the Church better make sure we're not making God upset!

God's thoughts will do three things. They will cause conviction. They will convince us. Or they will cause conversion. God told Noah to build an ark, something Noah had never done before. Do you know that God's thoughts will cause us to do something we have never done before?

When His thoughts convict, convince, and convert us, we will do as Noah did. Hebrews 11:7 says, *"By faith Noah, being warned of God of things not yet seen, moved in fear..."* (paraphrased). This is a time when faith and fear can be in the same place at the same time. This fear most times comes before faith. This type of fear is not a phobia; it is a reverential fear. A phobia will cause us to run away from God's thoughts; a reverential fear, however, will cause us to use God's thoughts, despite being fearful, to fulfill God's plan. God tends to ask of us things that are beyond our own ability because He knows that we cannot perform them without Him, and without His instructions and directions, which is again, more of His thoughts.

God gave Noah knowledge on how to build an ark. This is the power of God's thoughts. Some people say that the Bible was written by humans. Some say that the Bible is a book of fairy tales or allegories. Those who believe this haven't caught the thought that God is thinking toward them. You may not believe it now, but you will believe it in the Judgment. God will judge us by His thoughts that are written. *"For God so loved the world, that He gave His only begotten Son, that whosoever believeth in Him should not perish, but have everlasting life"* (John 3:16, KJV). This verse of Scripture says whosoever believeth in Him; however, here is the separation: "whosoever" believeth in Him doesn't mean "all" men. All men are not going to believe; however, the man who receives this thought shall not perish, but shall have everlasting life.

Second Corinthians 5:17 (KJV) says, *"Therefore if any man be in Christ, he is a new creature: old things are passed away; behold, all things are become new."* In this new life, God gives us a new tongue, a new song, and new thoughts. The Bible is given to God's people; yet it's also for those who are not God's people. Second Timothy 3:16 (KJV) says, *"All scripture is given by inspiration of God, and is profitable for doctrine, for reproof, for correction, and for instruction in righteousness."* No one knows what "righteousness" is but God. His righteousness comes toward us as a thought. Once we accept the thought, the thought turns into faith. It is only by faith that we will be inspired, learn His doctrine, accept His reproof, and be instructed in His righteousness. This is how we learn cognitively.

This reaction to the thought of God is called 'metanoia,' which means "the changing of our mind." The only way it changes our mind is by giving us a spiritual ear to hear. When God gave us the Holy Ghost, we received a new set of ears. These new ears are spiritual ears, which gives us greater receptivity at an even higher frequency. We operate on a frequency so high that no matter what storms of life we are in, we can still hear God's voice. Not only do we hear the voice of God, but we listen. Listening incorporates our minds. We can *hear* many voices at the same time, but we can only *"listen"* to one voice at a time. As people of God, one of the voices we can lean on reminds us to, *"Count it all joy when ye fall into divers temptations; knowing this, that the trying of your faith worketh patience. But let patience have her perfect work, that ye may be perfect and entire, wanting nothing"* (James 1:2-4, KJV).

Patience is a thought that gives us peace of mind. It calms our nerves and settles our hearts. The Apostle Peter had another thought that's connected to the verses in James 1:2-4. In I Peter 5:10, it says, *"But the God*

> God's thoughts may not be our thoughts, but God is determined and willing to share His thoughts.

of all grace, who hath called us unto his eternal glory by Christ Jesus, after that ye have suffered a while, make you perfect, stablish, strengthen, settle you." The way God accomplishes these things is that He sends us His Word that will perfect us, establish us, strengthen us, and settle us. All we get from God is His Word! When His Word becomes our thought to which we act upon, we will become an overcomer. Whatever comes, we will get over it. God's thoughts may not be our thoughts, but God is determined and willing to share His thoughts. And when we receive His thoughts, we owe God a praise. Hallelujah! *"I will bless the LORD at all times: his praise shall continually be in my mouth"* (Psalm 34:1, KJV).

David gave us the thought that should show up in our breath. If God's thoughts are not in our minds, neither will they be in our mouths. We can clap our hands and do our dance, but God wants to hear our praises. Our mouths open with, "Hallelujah!" A verbal expression of praise is one of the greatest extensions of our bodies because a praise is a thought, and a thought is "the" greatest extension of our minds. It can go backward and think of yesterday's blessing; it can go forward to think of the blessing that's coming. No parts of our bodies can go to heaven; however, the praise that comes out of our mouths can reach heaven and the blessings will come down.

True praise gets God's attention. Praise will make a space for God in our hearts, for God dwells amid the praises of His people. When Jesus' disciples were in a storm, Jesus showed up. The first thing He did was release this thought: *"Be of good cheer; it is I; be not afraid"* (Matthew 14:27, KJV). God tends to give us a good thought even when we are having a bad day or are in a bad place. This is why we must know the Scriptures, so we'll know that it is God who is speaking to us. Satan will never say to the winds, "Peace, be still." Satan comes with a storm to disrupt our peace. If we don't have Scripture in our mouths, we must send up praises out of our mouths. Satan can never receive praise in truth; that belongs only to God. Satan knows how God reacts to praise. Praise is a mighty weapon! If we have the thought that God is thinking toward us, it will cause us to give Him all the praise due to Him. Then we can rejoice and be glad!

CHAPTER 3
A GIFT CALLED THE MIND

"The mind is the element of a person that enables them to be aware of the world and their experiences, to think, and to feel; it is the faculty of consciousness, and to evaluate or process thoughts."

World-renowned psychologist Sigmund Freud was famous for inventing and developing the technique of psychoanalysis. He was credited for articulating and creating the psychoanalytic theory of mental motives, motivation, mental illness, and the structure of the subconscious. He influenced scientific and popular conceptions of human nature, saying that both normal and abnormal thoughts, along with behavior, are guided by irrational and largely "hidden" forces. These forces cannot be seen, but they are active in thought. Freud explained that the mind is where the id, ego, and superego all exist. He called the "id" the "dark" inaccessible part of our personality. Although hidden, the "id" will express itself in negative ways.

The "id" is an unconscious part of the mind that is driven by instinct and the pleasure principle. It's the source of a person's basic needs, drives and desires, including sexual and aggressive impulses. The "ego" is known as our idea or opinion and evaluation of ourselves, especially pertaining to our feelings concerning our own importance and ability. For example, when we say a person is "full of themselves," it's a reference to that person's ego, which is controlled by the "id." Freud says the "superego" is the part of the mind that acts as a moral conscience. It internalizes societal rules and parental values to guide behavior, telling a person what is right and wrong by producing feelings of guilt when they act against those standards. The superego is also considered that ethical component of one's personality that checks the impulses of the "id" and influences the "ego" to cause people to behave morally and normal. Normality is difficult to find nowadays.

We all have our own standards and beliefs that are, most times, governed by our family or friends. Now, out of all Sigmund Freud has said about the mind, he never mentioned the biblical function of the soul. Everything Freud has said about the mind, I call it "the soul of a man." I say this because when God caused man to become a "living soul," man received a living mind, will, heart, emotions, desires and consciousness. Some will say these components are not part of the soul. However, I believe all these elements are one package called the soul. The "power" of the mind can be used to achieve success, realize goals, and transform lives. Techniques like visualization, affirmations, and acknowledgement can all be used to direct our thoughts toward a desired outcome. For example, as thoughts run through the mind (the ones God puts in the soul), it can come to a solution or conclusion. Our mind must process every thought to determine our behavior. So, for one to come to a successful conclusion in the mind, it cannot be distracted by disadvantaged thoughts.

Originally, God gave us the mind so we can think and talk to Him in our mind, and even silently pray to God. I've found out that the best prayers are when we echo what God said or what God has written in His Word. God has never denied His own Word. His Word helps us make the right decisions or draw the right conclusions. In Ecclesiastes 12:13-14, the wise man Solomon gives us a hint on how this conclusion should be. He says, "*Let us hear the conclusion of the whole matter: Fear God, (reverentially) and keep his commandments: for this is the whole duty of man. For God shall bring every work into judgment, with every secret thing, whether it be good, or whether it be evil.*" Thus, our private thoughts—thoughts we've kept to ourselves—will be brought out into the open. We have the power to control our thoughts; therefore, we should align our mind and thought processes with the Word of God.

Our mind has the tendency to remember and recall the life we lived while in sin. Our mind can recall all the crazy things we've done. It's certain that sin will cause craziness. I am sure that most of us—if not all of us—wished we hadn't done some things while we were in sin. We knew better and did it anyway. If we decided to do or say something that was wrong, our conscience didn't bother us. Sin always starts with a "crazy" thought that initially sounded good. In fact, it will cause us to think we are right. However, there is no *"right"* in sin. Someone may label a person by saying that they have lost their mind, like a mentally deranged person who doesn't meet God's standards or society's standards. This is why a person can go into a mall, a school, a market, or even a church, and kill people before turning the gun on themselves. This person's self-talk is not meeting the standards of God, which is, *"Thou shall not kill."* The Bible says, *"As a man thinketh in his heart (which I believe is the deep dark portion of the mind), so is he"* (Proverbs 23:7). Sigmund Freud calls it the "id." The Bible calls it the "heart" of the mind. The heart is desperately wicked; who can know it but God?

This leads me to the topic of this chapter, "A Gift Called the Mind." A gift should never be stagnated in self-talk. It must be activated by God's thoughts and His Word. The mind is constantly evolving and rotating thoughts. The mind is like a mixer that blends everything into it, until it's all blended into one component. It's the same with our thoughts. Our mind can mix thoughts up, right and wrong. Like mixing oil and water, everything we think becomes one cloudy mess. If the mind is functioning properly, with God in the mix, He will help us prioritize our thinking, our behavior and our lifestyle. A stagnated mind is likened to our thoughts being in a blender, but the power cord isn't plugged in. It's just sitting there. It's not using what you have, and it's not plugged into God. The mind is a gift from God; therefore, we must use it with God in the mix so that we will become one with God. This will help us minimize unproductivity and prioritize our lives toward success.

I see the mind as a gift from God, who tells us how and when to use it; but, to keep it real, the decisions are always left up to us. This is what I call our "self will." Everything we do involves our will. Our will causes us to live or die. The Hebrew word for "will" is '*ratzon*,' which means one's wants or desires. Ratzon can be the volition or power of our will, to perform whatever our will may want. Watchman Nee, who was a 20th century church leader and a theologian, said in his book, *The Spiritual Man*, "Everything included in man's personality, that is, every element that constitutes him a man, is a part of the soul. His intellect, mind, ideals, love, stimulations, judgment, will, etc., are all parts of the soul." The Hebrew word for "mind" is '*lev*' or '*levav*,' which can also mean will, desires, emotions and even the heart. In the

Hebrew, the "heart" is considered the center of human beings' thoughts and spiritual life. It can also refer to the mind, heart, and will. Man is a spiritual being made up of three dimensions: the spirit, soul and body.

The mind—even the heart—would be the central command post to command all the parts of man's body, especially the joints and all other moving parts. Our body doesn't move until the mind says so. If our bodies move uncontrollably, something has gone wrong and it's not functioning properly. God's mind is like an incubator where babies (mostly premature) are placed after birth. The incubator nourishes the baby, keeps it warm and helps it grow so that the baby can eventually go home. Now, some may disagree, but man was like a baby in the incubator of God's mind or thought. God didn't create a baby; He created a fully-grown man. The man was like a baby who didn't know anything about life. God formed a home out of dust for the (invisible) man to live in. The original thought of God was for the man to grow and continue to improve, living a lifestyle that was in the image and likeness of God.

Our senses are sight, taste, smell, hearing and touch. We often say that our senses are something we cannot depend on to make a decision or come to a conclusion in life. When man sinned, he lost godly consciousness in his mind. When God asked the question, *"Where art thou?"* this question could have referenced us mentally and spiritually speaking. Man has allowed a disobedient, disadvantaged, and destructive thought to intrude into a place that God wanted for Himself, which is His gift to us called the mind. Man didn't unwrap the gift when it was necessary to use God's thought. We can never know the true gift of the mind from God until we unwrap it to see what God is saying and use His thoughts to make the right decisions. The gift God gave us, along with our mind, is the Bible. The Bible must be opened and applied. We can't know the power of the mind and the gift of God's Word that has the thoughts of God in it until the "dirt" or dust is removed. The more we open the gift and apply what God has said, the more the dirt or dust is removed, and the more we will appreciate the gift. It's like receiving the Holy Ghost; it, too, is a gift to assist us in our mind. Sometimes, the gift of the Holy Ghost is only half opened or neglected; sometimes, it's barely opened to the degree that we barely think like God.

When man sinned, he couldn't open the gift anymore. As a matter of fact, he may not have opened it at all. In one sense, man gave the gift back to God. When he gave it back to God, Satan stepped in. Satan caused man's mind to only be mindful of his surroundings and himself, even his ego. As

> The more we open the gift and apply what God has said, the more the dirt or dust is removed, and the more we will appreciate the gift.

a result, man's mind has the proclivity to only think that life is the accumulation of things for himself, or self-preservation, or his ego. But what does it profit a man to gain the whole world (or half or one quarter of the world) and lose his soul? The soul, mind, heart, will, desires, and emotions are lost when God is not in them.

God is so concerned about the man and his mind that He will always send His thoughts toward man. David asked a question in Psalm 8:3-4 (KJV), saying, *"When I consider Thy heavens, the work of Thy fingers, the moon and the stars, which Thou hast ordained; What is man, that Thou art mindful of him? And the son of man, that Thou visits him?"* God tends to visit us in the darkness of life, a time when we cannot help ourselves. We really don't see our value as God sees it. We were out of place, like a blind man in darkness. We will never know our uniqueness in darkness; it will only be known in God's light.

> *"O wretched man that I am!*
> *Who shall deliver me from the body of this death?"*
> –ROMANS 7:24 (KJV)

How frail and undeserving we are to receive God's thoughts. And yet, God is mindful of man. What a mighty God we serve! God wants to get us back to where we belong: in the mind or thoughts of God so man will be mindful of God completely. No other creation can receive thoughts like man. A tree is still a tree, and an animal is still an animal. The sun, moon and stars are all still the same and do not need a thought from God. Man is the only creation who needs a continuation of thoughts from God. Man is the heartbeat of God. John 3:16 says it best: "*For God so loved the world (the world represents the inhabitants of mankind on the earth), that He gave His only begotten Son, that whosoever believeth in Him should not perish, but have everlasting life.*" This is why God will always send the thoughts that He is thinking "toward" man, thoughts of peace and not of evil. Mankind never needed judgment until he lost his godly mind.

The invisible mind is where the invisible thoughts are. They cannot be seen until the thought manifests itself through the body, in word or deed. Colossians 3:17 (KJV) says, "*And whatsoever ye do in word or deed, do all in the name of the Lord Jesus, giving thanks to God and the Father by him.*" This verse of Scripture is a blessing of the gift of the mind to keep us mindful to always be full of thanks, unto the One who gifted us with a mind. First Thessalonians 5:18 (KJV) says, "*In every thing give thanks: for this is the will of God in Christ Jesus concerning you.*" If we are not in Christ, we will bypass the thoughts of being thankful. However, with Christ in our hearts, we will keep *the main thing* in our mind. "*I beseech you therefore, brethren, by the mercies of God, that ye present your bodies a living sacrifice, holy, acceptable unto God, which is your reasonable service. And be not conformed to this world: but be ye transformed by the renewing of your mind, that ye may prove what is that good, and acceptable, and perfect, will of God"* Romans 12:1-2 (KJV).

Romans 12:1-2 reminds us why we ought to keep God in our mind. It is only by the mercies of God that we are not consumed by the contrary thoughts of our mind. We can present our bodies—even our minds—as a living sacrifice that's holy and acceptable unto God, which is our reasonable service. This reasonable service is a spiritual service because it's not a fleshly presentation to God. My friend Elder Milton Andrew always says, "Take another look to see if you brought your mind to the altar of sacrifice." We cannot prove what is that good and acceptable and perfect will of God, unless God proves us. In the Old Testament, the priest could not put anything on the altar unless God approved it or requested it. God will prove us by what's in our mind and in our heart. That which is proven in the mind is only proven by faith. God has a dipstick called His Word to check the level of our faith. I have said it before, and I will say it again. Man is the only creation that God allows to prove Him, so God can prove them by searching man's mind and heart.

One of God's greatest blessings is His thoughts toward us. The rest of the blessings will follow the thoughts. Matthew 6:33 (KJV) says, *"But seek ye first the kingdom of God, and His righteousness; and all these things shall be added unto you."* We are not just seeking the place called the Kingdom. We should seek the King of the Kingdom *first*, for He and He alone will supply all we seek after that's in Him. Apostle Paul said in Philippians 4:19, *"But my God shall supply all your need according to His riches in glory, by Christ Jesus."* We get nothing from God unless it's by Jesus Christ. We use our mind for so many things, including figuring out our problems, making decisions and thinking about things we desire to do. These things may not be proven in time; but when we prove God, it will be in time and on time. We can prove God in sickness that He is a right-now doctor. We can prove God with our mind in times of trouble that He is a mind regulator and a heart fixer. God has a right-now answer to all our right "nows" even in adverse conditions.

Many times, we can't prove God until He proves us. God didn't turn Satan loose on Job until Job was proven by God. When God allows a problem to come into our lives, He will prove us to see if we will keep praising Him, keep loving Him and keep worshipping Him. God is trusting us with a problem, sickness and pain, storms and rains, and He knows we can handle it with His thoughts. He will not allow more than we can handle because our mind will stay on Him, not the problem.

In Matthew 25:14-15, Jesus gave a parable concerning putting more on a person than he could handle. The master gave unto one five talents, to another two, and to another one; to every man according to his several abilities (even their mindset); and straightway took his journey. Now, apparently, the master knew their mindset. We often trust folks when we know how they think or act. If I know you have the mind of a thief, a liar or a gossiper, there is no way I can trust you with a secret nor my goods. The talents were equal to three quantities of money. Money will create money if it is placed in the right hands. The parable says that the servant who received five talents increased it to ten, and the one who received two talents increased it to four. However, the one who received the one talent buried it. God knows what we are going to do with the talents or even the gift(s) He's given us. God knows our thoughts from afar off. The master must have used some wisdom. If he had given five or two talents to the person who only received one talent, he would have buried all of them, thinking the master was unjust. But again, Jesus is telling us that He knows our mindset and our abilities. Most times, God will use our abilities for His glory.

Money is neutral; it takes on the mindset of the owner. If we give a drunk some money, he or she will end up using the money for more drinking. If we give money to a gambler, he or she will use the money for more gambling. These individuals cannot return more money to the one who gave them the money. God has given all of us talents called gifts, especially our mind. All gifts are in the gift of the mind. When we have a mind full of God, we won't bury any gift God has blessed us with. I am convinced that gifts in the church can cause jealousy, strife, backbiting and even hatred because some saints have buried their own gift(s) and covet the ones that God didn't give them. It's because their mindset is on someone else's gift. Don't waste or lose the gift God gave you. Philippians 2:5 says, *"Let this mind be in you, which was also in Christ Jesus."* There is only one Jesus, and He has no competition. The mind that Jesus has was always to do the work of Him Who sent Him. When God gives us an assignment, He's looking for more activity of the same gift.

He sends more thoughts that He is thinking toward us, and He will trust you with His thoughts. With the thought, there is a call; all we must do is answer the call. The word "call" in the Greek is *"phoneo."* The person God calls is the only one who can answer. You can't answer my call, and I can't answer your call. God is personally calling us, and we will receive the power of the call. Statistics say that only twenty percent of the church has answered the call of the gifts. Eighty percent of the people just warm the pews, clap their hands, do their dance and say, "Amen!" God has never called a man, male or female, to just be comfortable in the pews. He has called all of us to be comfortable in an uncomfortable place. Sometimes, our uncomfortable places are in trials and tribulations, even in the storms and rains of life. Sometimes, it's because we have been disobedient. If the preacher preaches about sin, it may be uncomfortable to some; but you can be comfortable because you know you have not sinned.

Our mind will be convicted, convinced and converted. We will constantly receive, retain and repeat the thoughts of God. We will be like David, who said in Psalm 19:14, *"Let the words of my mouth, and the meditation of my heart, be acceptable in thy sight, O LORD, my strength, and redeemer."* God created our mind for Him to constantly dwell in. David also said in Psalm 119:11, *"Thy word have I hid in mine heart, that I might not sin against Thee."* The heart is the deeper part of our minds where, out of its abundance, the mouth speaketh. It's all about what we see and accept in our mind. The heart is also a place where the issues of life flow.

If we don't put God's Word on the issues, there is no telling what will come out of our mouths. Selah. I don't know about you, but I have never met a person who fully has the mind of Christ, especially being a saint. We still can think some crazy things and think it's alright, until God says, "You have lost your mind." We all have done some crazy things in word or in deed, even being saved. We thought we got away with it. Nobody may have heard it or seen it, but God did. God saw and heard everything. God is letting us know that our mind is not filled with Him or we are not mindful of Him like He is mindful of us. Every empty space in our mind that God is not in, is an opportunity for Satan to occupy.

When Satan sees an empty space, he brings temptation and doubt, and temptation doesn't like to pay rent. It is like a bad tenant; it will mess up our mind and will not care. We must be careful to not leave any room or vacancy for Satan to enter in. It is our spiritual responsibility to make sure the rooms, spaces and crevices of our mind and heart are all occupied by the Word of God or the thoughts God is thinking toward us. Hate, anger, animosity, backbiting, strife and malice should never occupy our mind. They will end up in our speech and actions, toward one another. We must remember that the thoughts God is thinking toward us is more than enough to fill all the rooms in our mind, even with an overflow. A spiritual mind is an awful thing to waste or lose. The Bible identifies several types of mindsets, and these only occurred after mankind lost his spiritual mind. We have the "human mind," where humans only think of themselves and self-preservation. It's either their way or the highway. Then, there is the "carnal mind."

I believe a saint can have a carnal mind regardless of how much they speak in tongues, dance, and shout in church. It could be a façade. They can be different people outside the walls of the church, to which I like to call schizophrenic. This is where a man has a split personality, and they don't know which personality is talking or responding. This type of mind is dangerous to the person because a carnal mind is enmity to God. You can have God's Spirit and still have a constant proclivity to do the things of the world, which is called carnality. God is a jealous God who has made it clear to put no other gods before Him. Lastly, no one wants a "reprobate mind." This is a state of mind that God has rejected sending His thoughts toward.

It's a mind that God knows will not receive the thoughts of salvation. God knows there is no repentance in this mind. *"Thou wilt keep him in perfect peace, whose mind is stayed on Thee: because he trusteth in Thee"* (Isaiah 26:3, KJV). Trust is the highest point of attainment in the Word of God, along with confidence in the thoughts of God. Truth is the highest point of faith in God's Word or His thoughts. So, if we put our trust in God's truth, our mind will be like God's mind. Our thoughts, desires and decisions will all align with God's. We know life is full of decisions, and it will lead us to God's expected end. *"My foot hath held His steps, His way have I kept, and not declined. Neither have I gone back from the commandment of His lips; I have esteemed the words of His mouth more than my necessary food. But He is in one mind, and who can turn Him? And what His soul desireth, even that He doeth"* (Job 23:11-13, KJV).

The mind is as valuable and necessary as our daily food. So, feed your mind with godly thoughts. When you eat God's Word with your mind, it will be sweeter than a honeycomb. Starve all thoughts that are contrary to God, like doubt and disobedience. Our mind is much like our stomach; it will enlarge itself if we keep on eating. The mind will digest the Word of God, which will nourish all parts of our body. Then, we will grow in the grace and in the knowledge of Jesus Christ. *"And we should be careful for nothing; but in everything by prayer and supplication with thanksgiving let your requests be made known unto God. And the peace of God, which passeth all understanding, shall keep your hearts and minds through Christ Jesus"* (Philippians 4:6-7, KJV).

> God's peace is beyond our comprehension. It surpasses our intellect, our education, and even the wisdom we think we have.

God's peace is beyond our comprehension. It surpasses our intellect, our education, and even the wisdom we think we have. It goes beyond all of these, with a direct aim towards our spirits. Once this peace is in our spirit, it makes a U-turn back to protect our mind and heart. If our spirit is not at peace, neither will our mind and heart be. We must know in our mind where our help comes from (Psalm 121:1, KJV). Sometimes we look up to folks who can't help us get up. Folks will say that they will be with you through thick and thin. However, when things get too thick, they thin out. Make sure you are looking up to the one God who created the heavens and the earth. God may not come when you want Him, but when He comes, you're going to want Him. Let's always remember God's gift of the mind and that it should always be filled with God's thoughts.

CHAPTER 4

THE CHANGING OF THE MIND

It is impossible to change your mind without changing your thoughts. Thoughts will come like a seesaw; some will be at an advantage, and some will be at a disadvantage. It is imperative for us to differentiate one from the other. Each thought will affect or change our thinking process, behavior and lifestyle. Every thought that comes to us may be good or bad. Over time, our thought process will evolve as we grow from childhood into adulthood. This change in the way that we think is a crucial part of human development. However, please understand that change doesn't mean better; but if we want to be better, there must be a change. Someone said, "The definition of insanity is to keep doing the same thing and look for things to change."

During the life-long process of changing, the only thing we can trust to remain the same are the thoughts of God for our lives. If we keep doing the same thing with the thoughts of God, part of our change is that we will have more of God, who is consistent in all His ways. Man started out with a mind that was an advantage to him; however, man allowed a disadvantaged thought to enter his mind, and it changed his mind about what God said. Man's mind is like a seesaw, up one day and down another. I am quite sure Adam heard the conversation Eve had with Satan. His mind became susceptible to the thought of Satan. In my own mind, I believe that once Eve took a bite out of the forbidden fruit, Adam was observing the whole thing. There were no outward changes in her appearance and there was no indication that something tragic had happened. Therefore, it was easier to conclude that what the devil (in the serpent) said was truth. It was then that the advantaged and disadvantaged thoughts began a short battle in his mind. One said, "Do," and the other said, "Don't." We know his mind must have said quickly, "Go ahead and do what the serpent said." It sounded better than what God said, which was not to eat of the fruit of the forbidden tree.

Our minds were designed to process and evaluate thoughts and determine our next steps. The mind can be a place of life or a tremendous loss of things in life, even the possibility of death. Adam chose the wrong "thought" and ended up in death both spiritually and, eventually, naturally. Oftentimes, we don't talk about the tree of life. On this tree was the ability to live forever without sin, which would have kept Adam alive forever. This Tree of Life would have enabled his mind to continually receive the thoughts of God and continue being in God's image. However, if Adam had been allowed to eat of the Tree of Life, in his sinful state, he would have lived forever as a sinful being, without any hope of eternal life. Therefore, as an act of mercy, God held Adam from eating of the Tree of Life. I say "an act of mercy" because He didn't want Adam or Eve to remain in the painful state of sin forever.

Sin is painful and destructive. What loving Father would want His children to live in a mode of pain and destruction forever? As a result, God put a flaming sword in the hands of an angel called a cherub. (Cherubim is the name for many high-ranking angels who are full of eyes, seeing 360 degrees. The name 'Cherubim' has two parts. The "Im" is an indication of many.) God used the many-eyed angel with a flaming sword to guard the Tree of Life, thus making it impossible for mankind to approach the Tree of Life and remain in a state of perpetual sin. I consider the fruit on the Tree of Life as a spiritual meal that was man's source of joy, peace, and contentment, which are fruit of the Spirit. When we live by them, everlasting life will be our portion.

When we get to heaven, we will see God and the Tree of Life. The Tree of Life represents the Son of God, which is the Word of God. My former pastor, District Elder Tommy Wood, used to say, "If you see God as His Word, when we get to heaven, all we will see is God and His Word at His right hand." The right hand is the hand of authority and distribution. I said that to impress upon you that Jesus is the Word of God, the Right Hand of God. God uses His Word as the primary source to change man's mind so he can return to God. God was in Christ, reconciling the world unto Himself. The Word of God is so powerful that it can convict, convince, and convert the minds of men receiving the thoughts (Word) that God is thinking toward them. In this chapter, the main thought is found in Romans 12:1-2 (KJV), which says, *"I beseech you therefore, brethren, by the mercies of God, that ye present your bodies as a living sacrifice, holy, acceptable unto God, which is your reasonable service."* God always does something for man first so that man can do something for himself in return. We cannot return to God unless we have His Word. Paul was speaking to saved folks by calling them brethren. How many of us who are saved still need a complete change of mind toward God? It's like one part of our mind is saved, but the other part isn't. It's like we want God to remain; yet some things that are not like God remain.

> When we come to church, we can't leave our mind at home.

The body includes the entire trichotomy of man: spirit, soul (which includes the mind), and body. God is saying, "Come to me and bring your body and "mind" with you." If we don't bring our mind, the body will not be a complete sacrifice, and no change will occur in the body. If we don't bring our mind, it will be a waste of time to present ourselves as a sacrifice unto God. When we come to church, we can't leave our mind at home. The whole trichotomy of a person must be present, ready to give and receive.

Our mind must be transformed into His likeness forever. Apostle Paul says, "*And be not conformed to this world (or as Elder Walter Stevenson says, "Be not 'conned' into the form of this world") but be ye transformed by the renewing of your mind…*" (Romans 12:2). The Greek word for transform is '*metashimatizo*,' which means "to reconstruct, remodel, or mortify." The word "mortify" means "to make major changes or to make a complete change." In other words, we didn't get a new mind; God wants to make major changes and complete changes to the '*same*' mind we had while we were operating in sin. Again, the transformation is up to us. God has given us the power to mortify the deeds of the body through the changing of the mind. It only takes place when we become a complete sacrifice. Philippians 2:5 (KJV) says, "Let this mind be in you, which was also in Christ Jesus." Jesus' mind was constantly focused on satisfying His Father because He Himself was the thought of God. The answer is keeping our mind constantly on the Lord. We keep the "yo-yo syndrome" in our mind when we try to focus on God *and* other stuff, too. Honestly, it's easy to have our mind on the Lord one moment; but then the next moment, our mind is on ourselves or the things of the world. That's why I say,

"God ain't through with none of us yet!" When we give our minds to God, He does the transforming by the washing of the water by His Word.

The Holy Scripture also represents water. We are not brainwashed; we are Word-washed. If God washes our minds, they will become whiter that snow. Now, that may be hard to believe, but Holy Spirit searches the mind and the heart. The Holy Spirit will find the dirt and show it to us so we can respond by saying, "Wash me, Lord, through and through; make my life all brand new, that I might be whiter than snow." The key to this washing is that it must be a sacrifice of our total self. Old Testament sacrifices were already dead before being placed on the altar. We must put our own flesh to death (spiritually speaking); however, our mind is not put to death. The mind is renewed. Flesh is put to death by ceasing from sin and carnal thinking, ceasing all activity that hinders us from being holy. We all need help in being and living holy. God's Word is what He uses to cut the flesh (negative and disadvantaged thoughts). Yet, God doesn't cut to kill the man; He cuts to heal the man!

> ... God doesn't cut to kill the man; He cuts to heal the man!

Presenting ourselves as living sacrifices is not a one-time experience. The altar is designed to be visited daily to put fleshly deeds and thinking to death. Because we are a living sacrifice, we can crawl off the altar at any time when things get too hot or when flesh begins to burn. However, if we stay there long enough, the experience of a renewed mind will take place. Our mind is primarily used to be a place of receptivity. We receive, retain and repeat words or thoughts—hopefully, the thoughts of God, so His words will become our daily activities. The ultimate purpose in life is God's Word. Let me say it again. Life's primary purpose is God's Word. Getting a Word from God is *life* itself. Everything that exists was created by the Word of God. God only put a special mind in man to be the recipient of His thoughts. The mind of an animal must be trained by man; however, the mind we have is from God and must be trained by God. If God can get your mind, then He's got you.

In the Old Testament, God would speak to men called prophets to deliver His thoughts to man. Hebrews 1:1-2 (KJV) says, "*God, who at sundry times and in divers manners spake in time past unto the fathers by the prophets, hath in these last days spoken unto us by his Son, whom He hath appointed heir of all things, by whom also He made the worlds.*" The Son is the Word of God.

Our mind must first be trained to know our inheritance. This knowledge comes by "cognitive learning" or by reading, observation, and application. Ephesians 1:17-20 (KJV) says it like this: "*That the God of our Lord Jesus Christ, the Father of glory, may give unto you the spirit of wisdom and revelation in the knowledge of Him: the eyes of your understanding being enlightened; that ye may know what is the hope of His calling, and what the riches of the glory of His inheritance in the saints, and what is the exceeding greatness of His power to us-ward who believe, according to the working of His mighty power, which He wrought in Christ, when He raised Him from the dead, and set Him at His own right hand in the heavenly places."*

This right hand of God is now our "High Priest," who can be touched by the feelings of our infirmities. Again, God is Elohim; He can be the Father, the Son, the Holy Spirit, and our High Priest all at the same time. In Matthew 11:28-29 (KJV), Jesus said, *"Come unto Me, all ye that labour and are heavy laden, and I will give you rest. Take My yoke upon you, and learn of Me; for I am meek and lowly in heart: and ye shall find rest unto your souls."* Going to the altar should be an everyday experience, whether it be at home, on the job, or at church. Anywhere we are in this world is an opportunity for an altar experience where we can present ourselves to God as a living sacrifice. This way, we make it easier to receive the benefit of God's thoughts.

The mind is the greatest activity of our heart, will, emotion and desires. It is the central part of the soul. That is why Jesus came to save our souls by quickening our spirits to new life through the Spirit of God. The Spirit of God is our "paraclete" that will lead us into all truth for the changing of our mind. Our mind is constantly laboring with thoughts that, oftentimes, we don't have answers for. We encounter certain situations that we can't do anything about. As a result, we're worried, stressed and even doubtful. That's why we must bring those thoughts under subjection, then rest in the Word of God. When God gave us His Word, He gave Himself to us, as well. If you've got the Word, then you've got God. His Word is truth; His Word will change our mind from being disobedient, hardheaded, and stiff-necked to being fully obedient. We often say, "Time changes things." However, time doesn't change *anything. We* change with time. We all get time; it's up to us what we do with it.

There are two Greek words for time. They are '*chronos*' and '*kairos*.' *Chronos* means quantitative time. It involves the time at the point our life begins until it ends. *Kairos* time is the qualitative time. It's the time that we spend with people or things we love and appreciate. It includes all the memories of life's experiences. If we love God, we will spend some quality time with Him, and keep His commandments through fasting, praying and meditating upon Him and His Word. We will not spend time on things that pose a disadvantage to us. Psalm 1:1-3 (KJV) helps us with this principle by saying, "*Blessed is the man that walketh not in the counsel of the ungodly, nor standeth in the way of sinners, nor sitteth in the seat of the scornful. But his delight is in the law of the LORD; and in His law doth he meditate day and night. And he shall be like a tree planted by the rivers of water, that bringeth forth his fruit in his season; his leaf also shall not wither; and whatsoever he doeth shall prosper."*

David revealed to us the thought of how *not* to spend our time within the first three verses of Psalm 1. The first verse explains three ways of how one is blessed. First, when they don't walk according to ungodly counsel. Second, when they do not stand in the way of sinners. And third, when they don't sit in the seat of the scornful. How can two walk together unless they agree? Birds of the same feather will flock together. Our counsel is *not* of man, but of God, for He alone is our wonderful Counselor! Standing in the way of sinners doesn't mean we are physically blocking them. It simply means we are not standing like a sinner stands. It means that we are not replicating their sinful ways. Our standards are different from theirs. We walk in a different direction with a different mindset. Although we may go through the same things sinners go through, the difference is that we will come out wiser, stronger, and better than before. As a result, we are headed toward God's expected end. We know we're going to end up in glory!

David continued with, *"nor sitteth in the seat of the scornful."* Scornful means extreme contempt, or rude, insulting, and disrespectful. Sitting implies being comfortable. We should never be comfortable in this seat. The writer goes on to say, *"But his delight is in the law of the LORD;"* and this is where we can use "qualitative" time to be with God in thought. And in His law doth he meditate day and night doesn't mean 24/7. It means spending some quality time with God during the day or night. It means

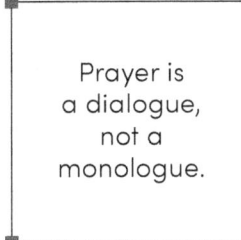

Prayer is
a dialogue,
not a
monologue.

meditating in the laws, precepts, and concepts of God. Meditating helps our mind to focus on a particular thing. It will cause us to turn the TV off, put the iPad down, and turn off the iPhone or any other distractions.

Prayer is one of the best ways to meditate. Prayer is a dialogue, not a monologue. Sometimes, we just cast our cares on Him and don't listen to Him "casting His cares upon us." It's not for God to always listen to us (and we know He will), but it's for us to listen to God and to know His will. Jesus said, *"Let Thy will be done on earth, as it is in heaven."* The earth doesn't change until man is changed. *And he shall be like a tree planted by the rivers of water;* this water is the Word of God that waters the roots of our salvation so the fruit of righteousness may grow and multiply. That bringeth forth his fruit in his season; his fruit is the fruit of righteousness. *His leaf also shall not wither;* this one leaf is known in the Hebrew as a seasonal, but a *generational* occurrence that indicates the continuation of life. There is no season of time that will cause our leaves to wither.

In the winter, the tree may look dead, but the roots are still alive, being nourished by the Word of God to bring forth the next season of leaves and fruit. I compare this tree to the "cedar trees of Lebanon," which is a metaphor of living a godly life. I found out that we can be in "time," but not in the "season" within our mind. This is because our mind oftentimes isn't prepared for the winter of trials and tribulations, disappointments, and discouragement. It's possible that we have not spent enough quality time meditating. We don't want our lives to be like the fig tree that looked good but had no figs. Jesus cursed it in this condition. *"I am the True Vine, and my Father is the husbandman"* John 15:1-2 (KJV). Jesus is the vine, we are the branches, and God, the Father, is the husbandman, also known as "the vinedresser." Jesus said, *"Every branch in Me that beareth not fruit He taketh away: and every branch that beareth fruit, He purgeth it, that it may bring forth more fruit."*

Anything in our mind that's not producing fruit is taken away. It will be a disadvantage for growth. "Purge" in the Greek is 'kathairo,' which means "to remove any undesirable thing." We can be saved and still have some undesirable things in and on us. *"Now ye are clean through the word which I have spoken unto you. Abide in Me, and I in you. As the branch cannot bear fruit of itself, except it abide in the vine; no more can ye, except ye abide in Me"* John 15:3-4 (KJV). Our mind cannot bring forth anything for God's purpose, unless we have the thoughts and the mind of God. *"I am the vine, ye are the branches: He that abideth in Me, and I in him, the same bringeth forth much fruit: for without Me ye can do nothing"* John 15:5 (KJV). We can do some things for our own purpose, but will it align with the purposes of the vinedresser of the vine? This alignment must be spiritual and mental. This can only come because of us meditating daily on God's Word.

"This book of the law shall not depart out of thy mouth; but thou shalt meditate therein day and night, that thou mayest observe to do according to all that is written therein: for then thou shalt make thy way prosperous, and then thou shalt have good success" Joshua 1:8 (KJV). When we are in Christ and Christ is in us, our prosperity will be a changed mind—the mind of Christ. A changed mind is a changed life! Everything Jesus did prospered for the Kingdom of God. Our souls are saved because Jesus kept His mind on His Father's thoughts so we can be connected to the vine.

CHAPTER 5
THINKING GOD THOUGHTS

In the beginning, God's thoughts were centered upon either creating something that never existed, or to restore, remodel, or regenerate something that already existed. God's thoughts are strong enough to change anything to the way He wants it to be. His thoughts are released from His mouth, and they cannot return to Him void. To think the thoughts of God, we must have His Spirit. One of the sure ways to know we are thinking like God is to be able to quote what He said. Again, this comes from cognitive learning by reading and memorizing His written Word. When we read His Word, it's like lifting God off the pages. The words of Scripture will resonate in our mind. After all, we are creatures of habit. Memorizing God's Word should be a habitual part of our everyday experience. I have said many times, "Get all you can, and can all you get." Get something that you can reserve and preserve something for later use.

We may hear a message and think it's not for us; but if we've "canned" the message, it will be useful for whenever it is needed in the future. It's like what I have said repeatedly: We must receive, retain, and be able to repeat what we have received. God's Word is spoken or written to us, and He wants His Word to be spoken and

> To *read* the Bible is fine; however, to *study* it is better.

written by us. My wife, LouAnne often says, "There's a blessing in the lesson, if we'll listen."

To *read* the Bible is fine; however, to *study* it is better. Studying is the only way to memorize the Word of God. Studying brings understanding and it is then that the Word becomes something that can be seen or spoken in our own lives. Studying must go beyond what is done in the pew. Homework is a necessity. I have found that it's always good to start your reading from the beginning, where God introduces Himself as the Creator. The beginning is where all His attributes to mankind began to manifest. The written Word is an affirmation and duplication of His spoken Word. No one knew what to write until God spoke it to them by "revelation." They could think the thoughts, repeat the thoughts, and write down God's thoughts. God's desire was for all men to hear His Word, to be able to repeat His Word, and to live His Word. God's Word is life itself.

Moses had to hear God's voice before he could write the "Torah" or what is called the "Pentateuch." These books contain the Law of God for Israel to remember and to live by. The first time the law was written, God wrote it Himself on a "rock." Anything that God writes or has written cannot be changed. Moses destroyed what God wrote on the rock, but he must have remembered what God had written because he was able to write it again, and the Word did not change. God does not have an eraser to remove His Word. God is His Word, and He does not erase Himself.

The law that God wrote on stone was a way of showing a miracle to Moses. This was the Lord's way of showing Moses and the people of Israel that they were dealing with a real, living God who could hear and speak to the people. Moses only "echoed" God's spoken and written Word that was given to him. Even the prophets of old did the same thing. Hebrews 1:1-2 (KJV) says, "God, *Who at sundry times and in divers manners spake in time past unto the fathers by the prophets, hath in these last days spoken unto us by His Son, (which is now the rock or written Word) whom He hath appointed Heir of all things, by whom also He made the worlds...*" If God had not spoken to those who were called prophets, and if they were not moved/inspired to write His Word, no one would know what God wanted man to know. This written Word was profitable for all men to know—not just the prophets and kings or noble men, but all men everywhere—whosoever will observe to hear what thus saith the Lord. The written Word keeps the consistency of God's thought, so all men hear the same revelation. I believe no prophet has ever told God what to write. They received what God wanted them to write by inspiration, and this inspiration caused personal conviction. God's Word was convincing, and they were converted and inspired to write what they heard. Second Timothy 3:16 says, *"All scripture is given by inspiration of God,* (God released what He was thinking toward them) *and is profitable for doctrine, for reproof, for correction, for instruction in righteousness."* God's righteousness would never be known if He had not released it toward man and inspired the prophets to write about it in His Word. This was all done so that man could be perfect (mature), and thoroughly furnished unto all good works, to the glory of God (II Timothy 3:17 (KJV)).

One of the definitions for "inspiration" in the Greek is *'theopneustos'* (theo-pneu-stos), which means, "God-breathed," "God has released His Word in or by His breath." The target of His breath is to bypass our fleshly mind, our own intellect and abilities, and enter our spirit. When God speaks into our ears, we receive spiritual resuscitation. As a result, man in the flesh could be quickened, and his spirit, which was dead in trespasses and sin, could be brought back to life. God released the Holy Spirit for the man to receive God's breath with His Word in it. When God releases His breath, He breathes His Word. This is why when the Holy Spirit was initially given, the people spoke in a heavenly language as the Spirit gave them utterance. The Word that was spoken was unknown to the speaker, but the hearers understood the Word that was being delivered.

On the day of Pentecost, they spoke "as the spirit gave them utterance." The Holy Spirit gives us receptivity or a special ear to hear what the Spirit of God is saying. This can be known as the transforming of the mind, to which we need His breath to continually breathe on and in us. When this happens, man is now able to think the thoughts that God is thinking. No one can think like God unless He releases His thoughts through His Spirit. We can read the Scriptures and not be inspired by them. However, if God breathes on what we have read, or what we're studying by faith, it will cause "inspiration" and again, inspiration will cause conviction, convincing and conversion.

Cognitive learning can also be described as cognitive receptivity from God. It fills up the memory banks of our mind to avoid forgetting the thoughts of God. Once again, thinking is the most active thing man does every day. We cannot stop thinking, no matter how hard we try. We say, "I don't want to think about that," but something else automatically takes the place of "that" with other thoughts. I've had songs in my mind that continually repeat themselves. Seems like the more I try to stop thinking about them, the more they keep coming. Sometimes, I don't remember all the lyrics to the songs. But the portions I do remember continue to play in my mind like a broken record. I googled this and found out that this phenomenon is called "earworms" or "brain-worms." It is like a worm that wiggles its way into an apple. This intrusion in our mind is typically caused by something we have recently heard or experienced. A thought or a song can get stuck in our mind, or a memory can be triggered that continues to play.

When we are faced with trials and tribulations, they, too, can trigger something that's already in our memory from the Word of God. In our consistent studying of God's Word, it wiggles itself into our memory. In every adverse situation, we can know what God is thinking toward us. The Greek word for "thinking" is '*skepsi*,' which means "to meditate" or "to say the same thing over and over" until it is settled in our spirit. Our spirit was created by God's Word. Our spirit needs God's Word to stay alive. This is why meditation is so important in the life of a believer. Meditation causes us to focus on one thing. The health and well-being of our spirit is the primary reason for meditation. The world calls it *yoga*. Yoga is known for improving our mental and physical performance, but the meditation I'm talking about is meditating on the Word of God to improve our spiritual thinking, which evolves into a Spirit-filled life. The Hebrew word for "meditation" is '*hagah*' (hag-ah), which means "the inward verbalization of thoughts toward God." In other words, inwardly, we are repeating what God has said or done and what He's thinking toward us. If we meditate on "grace," grace will occupy our thoughts. If we meditate on praise, we will praise God repeatedly until praise gets into our spirit. *"This book of the law shall not depart out of thy mouth; but thou shalt meditate (hagah) therein day and night, that thou mayest observe to do according to all that is written therein: for then thou shalt make thy way prosperous, and then thou shalt have good success"* Joshua 1:8 (KJV).

The best method of meditation is repeating what God says and what God says about Himself. God wanted Joshua to have more of the same victories and prosperity that Moses had. God wants us to have the same victories as the ones outlined in Scripture. God wants us to think as David thought in Psalm 27:1-3 (KJV):

> *"The LORD is my light and my salvation;*
> *whom shall I fear?*

> *The LORD is the strength of my life;*
> *of whom shall I be afraid?*

> *When the wicked, even mine enemies and my foes,*
> *came upon me to eat up my flesh, they stumbled and fell.*
> *Though an host should encamp against me, my heart shall*
> *not fear: though war should rise against me,*
> *in this will I be confident."*

"To eat up my flesh" means "to discourage me." The word "confident" means to "fully trust." Trust is the highest point of our faith toward God. The word for "trust" in the Hebrew is *'bittachon'* (bit - tach – hon), which means "to lay upon or lean on" and "to feel free." This carries the thought of us having given everything over to God, and now we are free of them. The confidence comes when we know we have a petition with Him and that He's heard our prayer and meditation. In Psalm 19:14, David said, *"Let the words of my mouth, and the meditation of my heart,* (our heart must think what God thinks) *be acceptable in thy sight, O LORD, my strength, and my redeemer."* When God hears something, He is going to do something. The only difference in God's hearing is that although He hears everything, He does not do all that He hears. Our prayers must have enough faith to reach Him. God will always respond when He hears His own words repeated by faith in the earth.

David said in Psalm 119:11, *"Thy word have I hid in mine heart, that I might not sin against thee."* That which is hidden (even in the heart) will always reveal itself. When sin tries to get into the heart of man, the standards of God will be lifted to stop the invasion. David wanted to receive more cognitive learning about God so he could think the thoughts of God. David sought God and inquired of Him for direction and instruction. In Psalm 27:4-5, David said, *"One thing have I desired of the LORD, that will I seek after; that I may dwell in the house of the LORD all the days of my life, to behold the beauty of the LORD, and to "enquire" in his temple."* David was seeking more of God's thoughts so he would not sin against Him. You cannot think like God and continue to sin. Yes, we know David did sin because he forgot what he had learned. He had a heart after God's own heart; however, he didn't have a heart "like" God. In Matthew 5:6 (KJV), Jesus said, *"Blessed are they which do hunger and thirst after righteousness: for they shall be filled."* Righteousness is a thought from God. It's the way God does things. Hungry folks seek fulfillment or to consume something to satisfy their hunger and thirst. However, David said, "O *taste and see that the LORD is good: blessed is the man that trusteth in him"* Psalm 34:8 (KJV). Hungering after righteousness will change our mind for us to think what God is thinking and to do what God wants done. That's when we will be filled.

My dad often told us, "Don't leave the table hungry; there was always more than enough." No one can set a table like God. He knows what our daily consumption needs are. As children growing up in my parents' home, when Mom set the table, we would often say, "I don't like what's on the table." Dad would tell my mom, "Just leave it there; they'll come back when the hunger pangs come." When we came back, nothing was left, and we went to bed hungry. Too many saints have gone to bed hungry because they didn't come to the table where the feast of the Lord is going on. The table of "meditation" is always ready when we are ready. When we are hungry and thirsty, we will come. On the table is the Word of God to feast on. When we meditate on the Scriptures, we will do as the prophet Ezekiel did. God told Ezekiel to eat the whole roll.

When he ate it, it was like honey in his mouth. Have you ever looked at food on a table, and it didn't look pleasing to the eye? However, when you tasted it, you came back for seconds? A verse of Scripture like, *"Love your enemies, do good to them that despitefully use you"* doesn't *look* good; but when we consume it, it'll be like honey in our mouth and we will find ourselves being sweet to our enemies. Verses like this will always take us to the place where God is. These verses give us the peace that God is thinking toward us. Thinking what God is thinking will bring us into His presence or a place where His glory dwells. God is omnipresent, meaning He is everywhere at the same time, but not His glory, not His weight, not His intensity. The omnipresence or presence of God will turn into a place of His "glory."

When we begin to think like God, God will always respond to what He has said. He watched over His Word to perform it. God is Alpha and Omega in the auspices of the concept of time. When we repeat by faith what He is thinking, it gives

God an opportunity to perform what He has said. Thinking what God is thinking is so powerful that once it gets into our heart, we will have a heart after God. That's when we become the "content of God's vision." The original thought of God was for man to be in His image and in His likeness. The fullness of life is just a thought that God is thinking toward us. *"Finally, brethren, whatsoever things are true, whatsoever things are honest, whatsoever things are just, whatsoever things are pure, whatsoever things are lovely, whatsoever things are of good report; if there be any virtue, and if there be any praise, think on these things"* Philippians 4:8 (KJV).

This kind of spiritual thinking is called "cognitive" spiritual learning. And the God of peace shall be with you, and this peace, God said, will give you an expected end. And this end may be pertaining to the eschatology of man, or man's final time on earth, but this end can cause many ends, on its way to the *final end*. This peace of God will cause an end to worry and stress. It will end suffering and sorrow, an end to disappointments and discouragement, heartache and pains that we just don't understand. This peace may end some friendships we didn't need and some relationships that were disadvantages to us. When we think what God is thinking, there will be a lot of ends before the *final end*. The wars and rumors of wars were all caused by a negative thought contrary to peace. That's why Satan starts wars with the saints—to take away whatever peace we have.

Satan and the world didn't give us our peace, and it's for sure that they can't take it away. Satan desires to sift us as wheat, as Jesus told Peter (Luke 22:31). I am sure we all can have the thoughts of God; yet, we do not retain them enough to repeat what Jesus has prayed concerning us. Sometimes, even with Jesus' prayers toward us, we forget His prayers. Jesus' thought toward Peter was for him to not "shift in the sift." Peter said, *"Lord, I am ready to go with thee, both into prison, and to death."* Let's be careful about what we promise the Lord; we just might do as Peter did when he followed the Lord from afar off. To follow Jesus, we must stay under His shadow and abide under His wings. Peter shifted in the sift and Jesus knew that he would. Jesus told Peter, *"The cock shall not crow this day before that thou shalt thrice deny that thou knowest me"* Luke 22:34 (KJV). Peter shifted from declaring that he would go with Jesus until the end to blatantly disowning Jesus (a thought placed in Peter's mind by Satan). When the pressures of life encamp all around us, we must remember the thoughts that God is thinking toward us and start thinking those same thoughts.

When Jesus asked His disciples, "Whom do men say that I am?" they responded by saying, *Some say that thou art John the Baptist: some, Elias; and others, Jeremias, or one of the prophets.* By this time, they had been with Jesus for three years. They had seen the miracles and heard His teachings; yet they still could not think the thoughts of Jesus. They walked with Him and didn't know Who He was. Peter, the one who was sifted as wheat, was converted by "revelation" of who Jesus was to strengthen the brethren. Through divine revelation, God gave him the right thought. Peter said, *"Thou art the Christ, the Son of the living God"* Matthew 16:16 (KJV).

To really know who Jesus is, I believe it only comes by revelation. Many have heard and read about Jesus and all He has done; yet many still don't know Him for themselves. Many don't know that He was God in the flesh called the Son of God. Sometimes, we can be with Jesus for a while and forget who He is. Jesus is the "I AM" of God. He is the real "I AM that I AM." He is the living Word of God. Jesus said, *"I am the light of the world," "I am the bread of Life," "I am the resurrection and the life," "I am the door to the sheepfold."* He is Emmanuel, which means "God with us."

Just before they entered Gethsemane, Jesus gave His disciples His thoughts toward them: *"Pray that you enter not into temptation."* Temptation will cause us to forget who Jesus is. How many of you know prayer will keep you from temptation if you don't fall asleep? How many times did the thoughts of God warn us not to do something and we did it anyway? We heard Him, but we didn't *listen* to Him. Sometimes (and life is full of sometimes), God's thoughts go in one ear and out the other. If we listen, we will mentally pay attention, and we will retain it.

Gethsemane was a challenge to even Jesus Himself because He was in the flesh. Here we learn the lesson to not let fleshly thinking override godly thinking. In this place called "Gethsemane," which was called "the olive press," this may have been Jesus' greatest challenge on earth. Sickness, blindness, causing the lame to walk, even walking on water and raising the dead were not challenges to Him. It was in Gethsemane where He asked God to "let this cup pass" from Him. The "cup" represented death. Jesus found Himself in a press. Our trials and tribulations are found in the "press." Whether we believe it or not, the "press" is the best place to think like God! It will press the anointing out of us. The assignment that God gives us can be challenging, but we must yield to His will.

Jesus prayed the same prayer three times: *"Take this cup away from me."* Nevertheless, He began to think the thoughts of His Father. *"Not my will, but thine be done."* It's in the press that we must remove our will so that the will of God will be done. Nowhere in Scripture does it say that the Father answered Jesus' prayers concerning the "cup." In some of our prayers, God is not going to say anything. God knew that His will was already in Jesus. Most times, when God doesn't answer our prayers like we want Him to, it's because He has already told us what to do. He is just waiting until we realize that His will is already in us. Therefore, we will yield to His will. Romans 8:32 says, *"He that spared not*

His own Son, but delivered Him up for us all, how shall He not with Him also freely give us all things?" This was Jesus' main purpose for coming as our redeemer. When we came into this world, I believe our main purpose was to do the will of God who created us.

Do you know what the will of the Father is? Even though He provided it to us, many times, we have asked for it to pass. When God didn't answer us, it was because He knew we knew the answer already. Sometimes, we think we are waiting on God when it is God who is waiting on us to obey His thoughts toward us. God is not going to think for us, but He will give us thoughts to think. It is best to think and obey the thoughts of the one who made us by His thought. He is the only one who knows what belonged to the thought. Remember, II Corinthians 10:4-5 (KJV): *"For the weapons of our warfare are not carnal, but mighty through God to the pulling down of strong holds; casting down imaginations, and every high thing that exalteth itself against the knowledge of God, and bringing into captivity every thought to the obedience of Christ."* We can think other thoughts that are only temporary in time; nevertheless, the thoughts of God are eternal and will give us His expected end. That end is to see His face in glory.

In conclusion, it is the Spirit of God who will guide us into all truth. Truth is where our assignment will be found.

Know the truth, and the truth will set us free to be who we ought to be in Christ. Keep your thinking clean by thinking the thoughts that God is thinking toward you. I pray something was said for all of us to receive and retain His thoughts. Let us ponder them in our heart so we will be able to 'repeat' them and act upon His thoughts in our lifestyle and through godly behavior. God bless you and keep you in His thoughts.

CHAPTER 6
CAN WE TRUST
OUR CONSCIENCE?

G od gave us a mind to think to evaluate, to meditate, to concentrate, and to dedicate our lives to something that will be an advantage to us. God gave man His thought for man to maintain his life on earth. According to most Christian theological interpretations, based upon the story of Adam and Eve, man didn't need "hope" before he sinned because he was already living in perfect harmony with God in the Garden of Eden. There was no concept of sin or the need for redemption, which is what "hope" typically refers to in a religious context. Therefore, the idea of needing hope came about after the fall from grace when sin entered the world. Now, man needs hope and anticipation. He needs to evaluate his thoughts to see if his thoughts are in line with God's thoughts. The hope that man has now has to be based upon what is now called "faith." Hebrews 11:1 says, *"Now faith is the substance of things hoped for, the evidence of things not seen."* Faith must be in man's consciousness to have evidence of things not seen. If *faith* is not in our thinking, we will only have consciousness of ourselves and the world around us. For when God gave man a mind, along with it, He gave us a conscience to always keep God in our mind.

The Greek word for "conscience" is *'syneidesis'* (syn-eide-sis), which means 'awareness' or 'to be aware, alert and awake.' It boils down to being a thought, or knowledge of something cognitively. In other words, When God created Adam and breathed into him the breath of life, Adam became a living soul (a man with a conscience, fully aware of himself and his surroundings). The prefix 'syn' means "with," and 'eide' is derived from the word 'eidenai' which means 'to know.' Finally, the suffix 'sis' means "action or a process." Our conscience is the action to know, and to be aware of something we already know, which will protect us from thoughts and actions we're about to do. Our conscience is known as a "compass" that gives us mental and spiritual guidance. The word "conscience" in the Hebrew is matzpun (mat-z-pun), which means something that is hidden. This refers to the hidden compass guiding one's moral decisions of what is right or wrong or even self-evaluation. Some call our conscience a "co-knowledge" or even a sub-conscience, which is known as "the part of your mind that stores and processes information without you being actively aware of it." It works on its own, without us asking for its opinion or advice.

Our conscience is in the mind. Sometimes, we don't know it's there. It just appears in our thoughts that seem to be uncontrolled. We cannot tell our conscience to be quiet; it will only bother us even more. It comes to remind us of something we have been taught or experienced, so we won't repeat the same mistakes. For this lesson, I compare a man's conscience with his heart. The heart is invisible and, again, I believe it came when man became a living soul. The heart is the deep emotions and desires of the mind. It is a result of things deeply embedded in what is right or wrong. So, in the reality of our conscience, it's a learned "cognitive behavior" of some sort of knowledge to help us decide our behavior, whether our behavior is right or wrong. This knowledge gets stuck in the memory banks of our mind even from childhood, and it started with our parents.

> No child is born a racist with prejudice against others.

Our parents taught us what they thought was right or wrong (whether it was right or wrong or not). Some parents have taught their children to hate a certain nationality of people or to even feud with their neighbors. This teaching enters their memory banks or heart, which is sometimes called their subconscious. It reacts without thinking about what we are about to do. We find ourselves treating others of another nationality as less than what they are, and our conscience doesn't even bother us. This incorrect knowledge evolves into an incorrect conscience, which results in incorrect behavior. No child is born a racist with prejudice against others. They're not born with the knowledge of how to treat people. Parents with good morals teach their children to love and respect everybody and to treat everybody right, or simply the way they want to be treated (correct knowledge/correct conscience). When we are about to do something that is wrong, we hear a voice from a correct conscience that says, "You know better" or "You better not."

When I was growing up, and I found myself misbehaving due to my bad conscience, my Big Momma (grandmother) would say, "You need to put some fire in that boy's back pocket!" In the household I was raised in, my parents did just that. It's funny how physical discipline can correct a bad conscience! Whenever my sisters, brothers and I went to church, Mom and Dad were our conscience. We were all aware of their presence. If we forgot they were there, we would soon find out. A deacon or a mother from the church would take us to our parents, and they would put some fire in our back pockets, or they promised that we would get the fire when we got home. My parents were promise makers and promise keepers!

There's an old saying that says, "When the cat's away, the mice will play." We all know when our parents were in church with us, we'd better not act up. Before we left the house, they would instruct us to behave or there would be some consequences. All they had to do was just look at us, and we knew "we'd better not." I am sure all of us have had a voice to speak to us, reminding us of what to do and what not to do. It may be our conscience speaking to us as a warning. In some cases, our conscience can encourage us to do the right thing. We can hear the voice of a mentor, a former teacher, or even pastors and Bible teachers give us correction that affects our conscience. Most times, we hear these voices when something is about to happen or when we are about to make a decision. Many times, we don't want our conscience to speak because we have already made up our minds to do something else. We can override our conscience, but our conscience never changes. It seems to work without us asking for its advice.

From infancy and teenage years to adulthood, we have a conscience that was taught to us by someone else. When we left our parents' home, we began to feed or retrain our conscience with our own ideas, precepts, concepts, and our own experiences. Many have left home and went to colleges and universities, and it changed what we learned at home and/or in church. Topics like evolution caused many to question creation or even God Himself. Sometimes, we are deceived by what sounds good to our senses, but not to our upbringing. If we don't know the truth or put truth on what we are learning, deception will take place. When a person embarks upon higher learning (trade school, college, university, etc.), they can tend to accept things that were not taught at home. Their knowledge of history, science, math and other curriculums are heightened, which changes their thinking and causes them to create their own opinions of things. Their conscience is then influenced by the way they see, touch, and understand things. When their thoughts are changed, it affects their consciousness because their conscience is activated by thought. As a result, thoughts that their parents or other influential people taught them begin to fade away from their memory, and they ignore a good conscience, or they avoid it altogether.

Many often say, "I am grown enough to make up my own mind," which really means, "I have a new conscience of my own." But on those days when we run into a problem that our conscience doesn't have an answer to, that's when we remember what our parents taught us and what we learned in church. Much like the prodigal son, while he was in the pig pen, his conscience brought him back to "sober consciousness" (he was reminded of home and came to himself). Our conscience will remind us of something that we already know. He remembered his father's house. His conscience convicted him, and, in that, he was convinced he could go back to his father's house, even if it meant returning as a servant. In the reality of the prodigal son, we all were in a pig pen called "sin." If we were taught to go to church by our parents, or to go to "God's house," our conscience will always remind us—even if we were in a backslidden state—that "you can still go back to God's house, even if only to become a servant." It doesn't' matter how low in life we go; we still have a conscience of where we are and where we need to go.

Now, let's get to the lesson. Where exactly did our conscience come from? Again, when God created the man as a thought and blew the thought into dust, man became a "living soul." This soul had an active living mind with a "hidden" (matzpun) conscience in it. It was hidden in the man's mind, and it brought about awareness. The man became conscious of God because God spoke to him. We would have never known or have been conscious of God unless He spoke to us. He is an invisible God; but because God spoke, the man became conscious of God, of his surroundings and of himself. This consciousness came from God. Man could see his surroundings and could see himself, but he couldn't see God who was hidden in him. By God being in his conscience, God wanted to influence the man's thoughts concerning his surroundings and himself. God gave the man instructions on how to live an everlasting life.

God planted two trees in the man's home, which was the Garden of Eden. The word "Eden" in the Hebrew means "a place of pleasure." Eden contained all the pleasures man needed—even to stay alive forever. God allowed Adam to name all things that God had created on earth; however, God Himself named these two specific trees to give man a choice of a lifestyle on earth. However, after the serpent influenced Adam's conscience, his conscience evolved into his own will against the will of God. I believe God named these two trees to give the man a choice simply because God had given Adam a living will when he became a living soul. What good is a will without a choice? If man were created without a choice, it would have been as though God created a robot. I would have never created a man who would eventually become hard-headed, disobedient, and stiff-necked. But the Lord said in Deuteronomy 30:19 (KJV), "*I call heaven and earth to record this day against you, that I have set before you life and death, blessing and cursing: therefore choose life, that both thou and thy seed may live.*" I am sure that most, if not all of us, know the names of the two trees I have referenced. One was the "Tree of Life," and the other was the "Tree of the Knowledge of Good and Evil." God placed these words in man's conscience: "*The day you eat of the Tree of the Knowledge of Good and Evil* (representing judgment), *you will surely die.*" Adam and Eve ate from the

Tree of the Knowledge of Good and Evil, and brought judgment upon themselves—and on all mankind, thereafter.

Hebrews 9:27 (KJV) says, "*And as it is appointed unto men once to die, but after this the judgment.*" Eve remembered what God said, even to the point of quoting His words to the serpent (who was Satan). We can quote God's Word all we want; but if we don't believe it enough to act upon it, Satan will become active in our conscience, and we will have a negative conscience or thought against God. I do believe that man can have an evil conscience. Now, what is an "evil conscience?" It is one that is full of self-serving disobedience, displeasure, adversity, animosity, revenge, hate, and oppression. It is worn out from self-effort and unbelief because faith has not been yielded to or has been clouded by disobedience. Faith is the consciousness of God. An evil conscience desires for us to do what is wrong constantly. Because of this desire, there is no guilt associated with committing any evil deed. As a result, man can do evil, and it doesn't bother his conscience at all.

Eve avoided the "consciousness" of God that was hidden in her because Satan's words were more alluring to her than God's words. Satan said, "You won't surely die." I've learned to never put a "won't" on God's "will." Eve ate the fruit of the tree, gave it to her husband Adam, and he ate, too. Neither of them knew what death was because they remained in a state that *appeared* normal to them prior to their fall. The real deception of sin is when one sins and thinks they've gotten away with their disobedience because they're still breathing. Adam and Eve believed that they had gotten away with their disobedience because they were unaware that their consciousness had been sheared from God. Whenever our conscience has been sheared/separated from God, it is no telling what will come out in our behavior. Despite the fall of man, God still had a plan for man. God chose a nation from the loins of a man named Abraham. The nation is called "Israel." The true meaning in the Hebrew for Israel is "God preserves" or "God rules." God gave Israel a law to maintain in their consciousness. This law would create a behavior that would be "correct knowledge," which with God, it is called "the truth." This consciousness called truth was to reveal to them that they had a "guilty conscience" and were not aware of it. We don't know how guilty we are until we know the laws of God.

A guilty conscience is void of God. The law would reveal evil in their mind and heart, or how guilty they really were. We can do wrong for so long that we think it's right. That's because our conscience doesn't bother us anymore. Israel had a fleshly conscience and God's law would be the means of removing their guilt by forgiving them of their sins if they obeyed it. God set up a system called the day of "Yom Kippur" or the Day of Atonement to where man and God would become one, even one in thought. An animal had to be slain, as God did with Adam and Eve, again only to "cover" their sins. In the process of time, Israel did not maintain the consciousness of God. In Deuteronomy 10:12-17, God did not receive their sacrifices because their "heart or conscience" wasn't right. They began to worship idol gods. Exodus 34:14 (KJV) says, *"For thou shalt worship no other god: for the LORD, whose name is Jealous, is a jealous God."* God has the right to be jealous because He is Israel's protector and provider. To be jealous is when you have done something for someone, and they don't appreciate it. God also has the authority because He is sovereign. The anger of the Lord was kindled against Israel because they gave His glory and their love to someone or something other than who it belongs to. As I often say, "Never make a god out of anything God has made."

Israel wanted gods that they thought would protect and provide for them. They desired a god that they could see and touch. All their idols came from their surroundings. They were manmade for man to worship. They made idols for their own pleasure, but all things were created for the pleasure of God rather than the pleasure of man. Revelation 4:11 (KJV) says, *"Thou art worthy, O Lord, to receive glory and honour and power: for Thou hast created all things, and for Thy pleasure they are and were created."* It's for sure that when we don't have a godly conscious, we will find pleasure in earthly idols and things. We will serve—even worship—idol gods that we can see and touch rather than serving the invisible God. We should never want to cause God to be jealous. He just might bring judgment upon us. God had given them a law that they never fulfilled, being that it was "weak" through the flesh or through their consciousness. Let's all remember that flesh is dust. It's the weakest thing on earth. Man let the weakest thing on earth destroy the strongest thing he had: a spiritual relationship with God. The law was to create righteousness and a holy lifestyle that God required of them.

The Apostle Paul said in Romans 7:12 (KJV), *"Wherefore the law is holy, and the commandment holy, and just, and good."* The law could not be fully achieved because of their sinful human nature. Galatians 3:24-25 says, *"Wherefore the law was our schoolmaster to bring us unto Christ, that we might be justified by faith. But after that faith is come, we are no longer under a schoolmaster."* This statement was for the Jews; however, it is applicable to all who are in Christ Jesus. Even the Gentiles (those of us who are not Jews) were under the "law of sin," which results in death. I have never known of a law that stopped man from sinning. We break laws every day (in thought or deed), which is a transgression against God's Word. So, death will be the result of the transgression of His law. The law is a biblical principle that states sin has a penalty that will cause a punishment. The result being death. We are all tempted to transgress against the law of God while being in Christ.

When our consciousness is earthly, it negates the consciousness of heavenly things. And it came to a point that Israel could not differentiate their consciousness from the consciousness of God. We can get so far from the consciousness of God that we cannot tell when He is speaking to our conscience, or if we are speaking to ourselves. Sometimes, we can do wrong for so long that we think wrong is right. This happens when our own consciousness is not convicting, converting, or convincing us. Sometimes, it's just a part of our human nature to have self-talk. We are "hu-man" and sin is in the "hu" or the flesh. It should never be in the "man" because the "man" was created in the image and likeness of God. We didn't know or realize how guilty our conscience was until we met the God who gave us a righteous conscience. Again, a conscience is like a compass; it is to be our guide in life. If we use our own consciousness, we will think we are going north when we are going south. No one is born with the consciousness of knowing where they're going in life. If you believe God gave us life, He and He alone knows the path that we must take. God has provided a 'conscience compass' called "the Bible" or His written Word.

So, the question is this: Can we trust our own conscience? I am sure we know by now that the answer is, "No." Although we may use consciousness of ourselves or our surroundings, it is for sure that if we use the written Word of God, it can and will change our conscience. All who are saved were saved by the written Word or by someone quoting the written Word. It influenced us enough to receive the thoughts that God was and is thinking toward us. When our conscience wasn't right, we needed to hear the Gospel of Jesus Christ to correct it. We learned that the Gospel is the power of God unto salvation, which changes our mind and our conscience. In some kind of way, the Word worked! Again, it convicted us, convinced us, and converted us. God did not remove man's mind nor his ability to think for himself. Man had an "incomplete knowledge" of his purpose. And man had no consciousness or an answer of how to get back to where he once was in "paradise." He may have known that there is a God using his memory, but his consciousness of how to get back to God as an "obedient" son was not available or active in his mind. It is a sad thing to know there is a living God, yet our consciousness is void of Him. Now, to go back to the beginning, which is where I usually go to help us know where everything began.

The Bible doesn't inform us on how Adam's sons knew how to make a sacrifice unto God; Adam still had in his memory of how God slew an animal and covered he and

Eve with the animal's skin. This was God's first display of mercy. God could have consumed them and would have been justified in doing that. From that point forward, and for a long while, all sacrifices were to only *cover* man's sin, not to *remove* sin. Sin is in our human nature; we must let God deal with it. Some sinners think because they bring God an offering or a sacrifice, they will automatically be alright or in good standing with God. That's because their conscience doesn't bother them. This is much like Cain, who is the oldest son of Adam and Eve. Cain had a self-willed or rebellious conscience. However, Abel, who is Adam and Eve's second son, had a consciousness toward God. Abel's consciousness was to satisfy God by slaying an animal and bringing it to God as a sacrifice. When God saw the blood of the sacrifice, God covered Abel with His mercy. This offering only covered him; it was incomplete because it didn't remove his sin. On the other hand, Cain didn't have the consciousness of God to bring God a sacrificial animal. He brought something that God didn't require. Anytime we bring God something He didn't require, it is called a "Cain offering." This offering is a vain effort to satisfy God. Cain brought God something of the earth. The earth was cursed because of Adam, and nothing that is earthly can satisfy God unless He requires it. Therefore, Cain's sacrifice was rejected. Because his offering was rejected by God, he turned his anger toward his brother, Abel. Sometimes (and life is full of sometimes), when we can't take things out on God, we tend to take our anger out on a brother or sister. Again, this begs the question, "Can we trust our *own* conscience?"

In my research, I found out that the name "Cain" represents the things we have gathered or done in the past. Cain's name carries the thought of bringing God what you have achieved to satisfy your own consciousness. When we were in sin, God's mercy and grace went after us. While we were yet in sin in the past, God commended His love "toward us." In other words, when God went after Cain, I believe this was the first time God showed man His grace called reconciliation. God didn't have to go after him. Reconciliation was not to dismiss his sin, but to remind him of his guilt. God's grace will reveal how guilty we really are. God told Cain, *"If thou doest well, shalt thou not be accepted? and if thou doest not well, sin lieth at the door"* (Genesis 4:7, KJV). That door is the door of man's heart.

Whenever disobedience enters the door of our heart, we need a spiritual heart transplant, or our conscience needs to be changed. Cain's heart hardened and he couldn't take his anger out on God. So, he took it out on his brother Abel because his sacrifice was acceptable unto God. This type of jealousy will always lead to destruction. In Song of Solomon 8:6, King Solomon said, *"Jealousy is cruel as the grave."* Our conscience is susceptible to negative thoughts. In Proverbs 14:12 (KJV), it says, *"There is a way which seemeth right unto a man, but the end thereof are the ways of death."* When we make one wrong conscious decision, it can lead us to many wrong decisions, and life is full of decisions. Now, a conscience can be a conclusion that will determine our next step in life or what matters in life. Ecclesiastics 12:13-14 (KJV) gives us what matters concerning life: *"Let us hear the conclusion of the whole matter: Fear God, and keep his commandments: for this is the whole duty of man. For God shall bring every work into judgment, with every secret thing, whether it be good, or whether it be evil."* This includes the thoughts of man's conscience.

Remember, man wasn't supposed to ever have a judgment concerning life; that all changed when he ate from the tree of judgment. Hebrews 9:27 (KJV) says, *"And as it is appointed unto men once to die, but after this the judgment."* Sin caused judgment and death; however, today, man is more consciously involved in the consequence of death. We have life insurance and wills, and neither of these insures life. But when we heard the Gospel of Jesus Christ, He would be our only insurance of life and even abundant life. Most people have heard the Master saying, "Come and dine," which influenced and infiltrated our conscience, letting us know that we had an incomplete conscience. In that, we realize our conscience was a guilty conscience because we were in sin. Again, it convicted us, it convinced us, and it converted us. And we did what they did on the day of Pentecost. We were baptized in the name of Jesus Christ, and we were filled with God's Holy Spirit. First Peter 3:21 (KJV) says, *"The like figure whereunto even baptism doth also now save us* (not the putting away of the filth of the flesh, but the answer of a good conscience toward God,) *by the resurrection of Jesus Christ."* Baptism doesn't save the flesh because the flesh has an appointment with death. Baptism is the first physical step of change in our conscience after repentance. It is called metanoia, which means "the changing of the mind." This evolves into the changing of our conscience.

We must be confident that the Gospel of Jesus Christ is the power of God unto salvation. Our conscience must be trained by the renewing of our mind. Yet, we still have the old human mind and His conscience. The question becomes, "Which one are we going to choose to be—the compass or guide for us in life's journey?" God gives us the greatest hint: Choose eternal life, for this life will be the consciousness of God. If we sin, even with the Holy Spirit in us, our conscience will always remind us to repent. Repentance is not just to be remorseful, but it means to turn from the sin and walk away. When we turn, we are turning to the power of God to help us walk away and never do that same sin again. David is our perfect example of this. When he repented of sin, he never did that same sin again. When we repent, God will give us the power to not sin again. God gave us the Holy Ghost as a compass to lead and guide us into all truth. Truth is the main element to avoid the consciousness of the old man. When the old man's conscience reminds us of what we used to do, our godly conscience will respond. "I am not what I ought to be, but thank God, I am not what I used to be." Second Corinthians 5:17 says, *"Therefore, if any man be in Christ, he is a new creature: (or creation) old things are passed away; behold, all things are become new."* This newness is a constant change in our conscience and in our behavior. When things are turned upside down and turned around, our godly conscience says, "The Lord will make a way somehow." When we come to the end of the rope of life, and we think we are not going to make it, our godly conscience will give us "somehow hope" so we can tie a knot on the rope to still hold on.

Weeping may endure for a night, but our godly conscience will somehow let us know that joy is coming in the morning. When our hearts are overwhelmed, our godly conscience says, "I'll lead you to the rock that's higher than you are." This godly conscience is hidden in us. It can only be seen when we make the right decisions according to God's Word. That's all life is about; it's a "thought" in our consciousness that will lead us to life or death. I hope this chapter will remind us that a godly conscience pleases God because it reflects God's thoughts. I pray that something was said that will enhance your ability to always be conscious of God, for He said, "*I will never leave you nor will I forsake you*." This is one, if not the greatest, comforting words that God is thinking toward us. May God bless you to use godly conscience in every decision in your life.

CHAPTER 7

Do Not Conform
to the Storm

Storms are not necessarily external. Many times, storms are *internal*, and sometimes, internal storms may cause external storms. Sometimes, the storm can be inward and can overflow outwardly to a friend, co-worker, your children, or your spouse. If we conform to the storm inwardly, we cannot transform into the peace that God promised. The best way to not be conformed is to use the thoughts of God. Jesus said, *"Love ye one another, as I have loved you."* You must use the same thoughts He is thinking toward you, toward one another. Once you've done this, it'll help to remove the anger and the differences of opinion that can keep people at odds with each other.

Anger has the tendency to stir up even more anger. Proverbs 15:1-2 says, *"A soft answer turneth away wrath: but grievous words stir up anger. The tongue of the wise useth knowledge aright: but the mouth of fools poureth out foolishness."* I had a friend who always was mad and negative. One day, we sat and talked for a long while. When I left, I left with the same spirit he had. On my way home, someone cut in front of my car. I chased the driver, yelled at him, and used some four-, five-, and six-letter words! I wasn't saved at the time. I experienced *road rage*. He apologized and went on his way. But I thought, *Why am I so angry?* Then I realized I had picked up the same spirit as my friend.

Angry spirits are contagious. It's like a virus that you catch when you're around other people. My friend's storm became my storm, but I thank God everything turned out all right. We can hurt one another with our storms of hatred, animosity, anger, jealousy, and backbiting. Our tongue can write a check that our bank account cannot pay. We are living in a time that people are killing others just because they looked at them. I am not talking about folks in the world, like how I was when I did what I did. I am talking about saints and church folks who have inward storms and have conformed to their storms.

We are living in a time when folks are leaving the church because the church didn't help them with their storms. We don't realize that we can run from the bear and meet the lion. Some say things like, "The church hurt me," "The pastor didn't preach the kind of message that I needed," "The deacons were mean," and "The mothers of the church told me my dress was too short/or my suit was too loud." These are many of the reasons people have stopped coming to church. However, folks can mistreat us on the job, but that doesn't stop us from coming back to the job. Sometimes, we can encounter a person in the church who's also dealing with a storm. When two storms meet, the results may be catastrophic. Life will have many storms; but it's how we handle them that's important.

Sometimes, external and internal storms can overwhelm us to the point that we don't know what to do. But if we learn to trust God in our storms, He will be our shelter in the time of storms. This shelter is the thoughts God is thinking toward us. His thoughts have the power to calm any storm inwardly and outwardly. A storm is most times identified externally by a strong wind, a hurricane, tornado, heavy rain or snow. There is turbulence in the atmosphere. As a result, we shut ourselves in our homes or in a building for safety. Whenever we're going through storms like trouble, trials and tribulations, we shut ourselves in like a turtle in its shell. We don't want to talk to anyone, and we don't want anyone to talk to us. When friends or family turn their backs on us, this can cause an inward storm because we thought they loved us until the end. The end came when we disagreed. I often say, "Wise men differ, but fools fall out." Sometimes, we must agree to disagree to keep peace. We must remember that we have a God who loves us more than we love Him, and a God who loves us more than we love ourselves. He knows how to calm the storm—

externally and internally. Many times, God will calm the storm that's in us first before He calms the storm that is raging outside of us.

One of the greatest storms we can have is *fear*. Fear tends to cause us to lose our equilibrium. Fear will cause worry, or stress, and will put our nerves on edge. In this chapter, I want to use one of the familiar stories of the Bible that's found in Matthew 14:22-33, where Peter walked on a stormy sea. Let me elaborate on something that will help bring clarity to our lesson. I do believe that there would not be any storms, hurricanes, tornadoes, and turbulent weather inwardly nor outwardly, if man had not sinned. Some of you may not believe that; however, we don't read of a rainstorm until one came during the time of Noah. Water always came from under the earth to water the earth. We don't read of a rainstorm until the thoughts of man were continually wicked. I'm referring to the internal storms we're now facing due to disobedience. Disobedience will cause God to send an outward judgment called a storm. Man wouldn't have to face internal trials or tribulations, troubles and problems in life if man would've listened and applied the thoughts of God. And again, there would not have been any storms in the atmosphere if man had not sinned. Storms in the atmosphere are usually a judgment called by God. Storms in the atmosphere can't be controlled by man. This is because God never gave man dominion of the sky or the heavens. A storm (such as a thunderstorm, etc.) can mess up your day. Sometimes, we conform to that storm. We find ourselves not wanting to go to church because it's raining or snowing; but here again, we go to work despite inclement weather. Common sense would tell you not to go out in a storm if it's a tornado or hurricane, or some other severe storm that can be dangerous and harmful. Sometimes, the inclement weather can affect how we feel or impact our mood, especially mentally.

Again, I believe a storm can be a judgment call by God— not all of them, but those storms that are the direct result of man's sins. I said before that man does not receive a judgment from God until he has sinned. This is because man ate from a forbidden tree and brought judgment upon himself and to all men. Man sinned because of a thought contrary to God's thought, and man became fearful of God. He had what we call a "phobia." It's a type of fear that causes one to run away from what he/she feels may do harm. If Adam had the fear called "reverential fear," which is respect, honor and love for God, then instead of running away from God, he would've run *to* God. Man's fear (phobia) caused him to run and hide himself from a loving God. There was a storm of fear within man, and he couldn't calm the storm by himself. Proverbs 1:7 says, "*The fear* (reverential) *of the LORD is the beginning of knowledge: but fools despise wisdom and instruction.*" God's knowledge is one of the most important things in life. Knowledge is a thought that will give us the advantages or disadvantages of life. But God's thoughts will always give us an advantage that leads to a better life. When you know the right thing, there is no fear. When we use God's thoughts that He is thinking toward us, they will give us wisdom, and this wisdom is *faith*.

Fear (phobia) cannot be in faith, but faith can be in fear (reverentially). For example, Hebrews 11:7 says, *"By faith Noah, being warned of God of things not seen as yet, moved with fear, (reverentially) prepared an ark to the saving of his house; by the which he condemned the world, and became heir of the righteousness, which is by faith."* As a point, I never read where Noah told the people, "It's going to rain." We may infer that he did, but nowhere in Scripture did Noah speak to anyone about what God said. God knew He was only going to save eight people: Noah, his wife, their three sons, and their wives. God also purposed to save some of the animals. God was going to save eight souls because eight represents new beginnings.

The ark was a metaphor of the Church. Only those who are in Christ, or in the Church, which is the ark of God, will be saved from the storm that hasn't been seen yet. I consider the widespread evil operating in this world as being a great storm, and these storms caused by the evil entities of this world are only going to get stronger. Jesus said in

Matthew 24 that we will hear of wars and rumors of wars, nations against nations, famines and pestilences, earthquakes in diverse places. But, when we see these things, the end is not yet. How much worse can this world endure before somebody trusts God? Jesus also said these things are only the *beginning* of sorrows. We will hear the saints say, "Come now, Lord." Only a few will be saved from the evil of this world to start a new beginning. We are only in Christ by grace through faith, and not of ourselves. It is a gift of God. Faith that will float our boat through the world to get us to the other side, which is glory.

So, let's get to the lesson. It's found again in Matthew 14:22-33. Now, prior to this story, Jesus had performed a miracle by feeding five thousand men, plus women and children, with two fish and five loaves of bread. His disciples gathered the leftovers, which were twelve baskets full. There were twelve disciples, so each disciple had a basket of miracles for themselves. Jesus constrained them to get in a boat and go to the other side. Now, when Jesus constrains a person, it's like He's giving them a command and, even better, it's like He's making them a *promise*. Most times, Jesus doesn't give the details of the promise. Someone said, "The devil is in the details." If we spell "devil" backward, it will spell l-i-v-e-d. The devil wants us to live life backward. The devil wants us to live in the storms of sin once again and to never reach the expected end God has for us. I am sure most of us have had experience with the devil or his demons. When we run into a problem, we question the promise because the problem doesn't look like promise.

When Jesus' disciples got into the boat to go to the other side, they met a detail of the promise that Jesus hadn't informed them about. Out in the sea, a storm arose, and the boat was tossed to and fro. Has anyone ever been tossed to and fro, even with a promise from God? When God gives us another day, He doesn't promise us that there won't be some heartaches and pain, sickness, death, and even fear in that day. However, the fear that the disciples had that night was a phobia. They saw a figure walking on the waves of the stormy sea. Now, I know this is hindsight, but I wonder why the disciples didn't look at the miracles in the boat, which were the twelve baskets of fragments. The baskets represented the power and ability of Jesus. Sometimes, we look at the storm more than we look at the blessings we already have. The blessing should remind us that since Jesus has performed one miracle, He can perform yet another one. God is the same yesterday and every day, even during storms. If He did it once, He is well able to do a miracle again. He can and will do it again! Jesus comforted them with these words: *"Be of good cheer; it is I; be not afraid."* How many of you know God must calm the storm that's in us before He calms the storm that we are in? Jesus sent the thought of peace that He was thinking toward them. This peace is the same peace God is thinking toward us. In this situation, Peter asked a question that didn't have faith in it. Faith is the substance of things hoped for, and Peter didn't have any substance of hope. He said, "*Lord, if it be You, bid me to come.*" Peter said, "if;" but if he had looked at the miracle of the twelve baskets of fragments that were in the boat, he should've had faith in the one who was outside the boat. He should have said, "*Since it is You, bid me to come.*"

Sometimes, fear will cause us to put an "if" in what God says or has promised. "If" in this situation means a conditional clause on a condition. Peter was asking a conditional question. This is the question a person would ask who may have a little faith, but not enough faith. It's like saying, "Lord, I am sick. Heal me "if" You can." Jesus had told His disciples to go to the other side. But they were prevented from going to the other side due to being stuck in a storm. As a result, phobia set in. Fear can also keep you from going to the other side.

I am reminded of 1 John 3:2 that says, "*Beloved, now are we the sons of God, and it doth not yet appear what we shall be: but we know that, when he shall appear, we shall be like him; for we shall see him as he is.*" We have not yet made it to the other side, so let's not allow fear to stop us from being who we shall be. Peter asked a question that had no faith in it. Jesus must have realized Peter didn't have any faith; but we know faith cometh by hearing and hearing by the Word of God. So, Jesus sent Peter one word that was enough to create faith. The faith Peter needed was only one word. All we need is one word from God to do the impossible. I believe Peter wasn't walking on the water; he was walking on the Word of Jesus, which was simply, "Come." If we put the faith that God gives us in between ourselves and our storms, the storm will be under our feet, and we won't sink. Peter got out of the boat and began to walk on the Word of Jesus through the raging sea. When God tells us to come, please keep stepping. Fear may set in; but by faith, we will reach Jesus.

There is power in the word "come." Faith will put pep in your step and glide in your stride. However, the faith Peter had didn't last very long. Someone once said, "It's not how we start, but how we finish." We must keep the faith until we get to Jesus. Faith is a gift from God. The more we open the gift, the more we will get closer to Jesus. That is the main purpose of faith—to get us where Jesus is. Peter stopped walking by "faith" and began to walk by "sight." Where we "look" with our sight is where we are going to go with our feet. Peter took his eyes off Jesus and began to conform to the storm. Peter cried out, "Lord, save me!" Jesus came to his rescue and lifted him up out of the sea.

I believe Jesus was obligated to rescue Peter because He had constrained all the disciples to go to the other side. Jesus kept His word to get them all to the other side. God will respond to everyone who cries out to Him. There will be times in our spiritual life that we will see God making a way out of no way to lift us up again. God will keep us from falling, for He wants to present us faultless before His presence with exceeding joy. When you cannot help yourself, or even when you don't want to be kept by God, He is a keeper.

I don't know about you, but Jesus has promised me that He will get me to the other side if I keep the faith. I now understand the question, "If it had not been for the Lord on my side, where would I be?" We would have been consumed in the storms of life. We're often in some sort of storm, from the White House to the doghouse. However, the mindset that we all need while we're in the storms of life is that Jesus will keep us, so we won't conform to the storm. We will not be conformed to the world, but we will be transformed by the renewing of our minds.

We are living in perilous times, but we don't have to let the perilous times live in us. God will float our boat by faith. In every storm, we must remember greater is He that's in me than he that's in the worldly storm. We must remember what David said in Psalm 27: *"The LORD is my light and my salvation; whom shall I fear? The LORD is the strength of my life; of whom shall I be afraid?"* We can stand on the promises of God that we will get to the other side. When the enemy comes in like a flood, God will lift a standard. However, we must be standing on the standards of God for Him to lift up the standard. Daniel 11:32 says, *"And such as do wickedly against the covenant shall he corrupt by flatteries: but the people that do know their God shall be strong, and do exploits."* One of the meanings of "exploit" is to take advantage of a situation in a disadvantaged situation. Use the thoughts that God thinks toward you, and you will not conform to the storm.

CHAPTER 8

USING THE RIGHT LANGUAGE

A language is a thought expressed by our mouths, which is simply the communication of words. Language usually identifies a "nation" with the same speech or what is called the same tongue. A language is words said to one another to establish an understanding that can cause an agreement or disagreement. Language originates in the mind. The mind has been trained to speak a certain language that's common to its environment. It can also create a culture, one with the same beliefs and customs. Language, at its worst, can also cause division.

First Corinthians 1:10 (KJV) says, *"Now I beseech you, brethren, by the name of our Lord Jesus Christ, that ye all "speak" the same thing, and that there be no "divisions" among you; but that ye be perfectly joined together in the same mind and in the same judgment."* The word *judgment* in this context means a decision, which can cause a division. We must all agree with the decisions Christ has made. This verse can and will separate a lot of people, even in those who believe in the Gospel of Jesus Christ. We all think differently. We have different opinions and ideas concerning the same subject. Also, our judgments will be different, either by our conscience or perception. In the verse we just read, the Apostle Paul is not talking about speaking in an unknown tongue here (although speaking in tongues has caused us to be a "Chosen Generation" and a "New Nation"). What he was referring to was that we should have the same speech, mind and judgment. God called us out of darkness for the purpose of speaking to God and one another in "His" language. We can't talk to each other in an unknown tongue, or it will cause a real separation. Speaking to one another in love is the language of God.

Apostle Paul wanted us to understand that whatever language we speak should be based on what God says. We can't speak the language unless we have the same mind and the same judgments. It is imperative that we receive the same thoughts of God, the ones He's thinking toward us. God wants man to speak to one another as He speaks to us. It would be impossible for man to use the language of God and not have the mind of God. We all must have His Spirit. God's Spirit is what causes man to have the same spiritual language.

The only way to have God's mind is by having the same thoughts of God. Now, if anyone speaks English, Japanese, Spanish, German, French, Greek or Hebrew, we can still speak the same thoughts of God, but in different languages.

The key to any language is that God can speak in *all* languages. God has a language that all men can understand. There was one language and the same speech in the beginning. Because man wanted to build a tower to reach heaven, God came down, confused their language and gave them different languages at the Tower of Babel, which, at that time, was in a place called Shinar or Babylon.

According to the Bible, after the confusion at the Tower of Babel, God divided the people with three different languages. I believe there were three basic languages. There could have been more, but I believe there were only three because of the three sons of Noah. But in the process of time, man began to speak more than three languages and various types of dialects. God can speak in any dialect of man so men can come to the knowledge of God and know that He is the Creator of all things that exist. He can speak directly to man. In the process of time, man desired to serve a god that could not speak. We call these "idol gods." Even if their gods could speak, they still didn't have God's thoughts. Language is a by-product of thought. We cannot hear the thought until it is spoken in a known language or speech. God's thoughts cannot be seen either. Once received, these elements will evolve in our language and speech. The thought of God is peace, to give all men an expected end. This type of language will end in peace. Even after an argument or disagreement, it tends to give peace after a broken relationship or marriage. I found out it will give you peace after a loved one passes away.

No man knows when the end will be or when the end will end. God's end will always end up at the expected end called *peace*. God said, *"My thoughts are not your thoughts and My ways are not your ways."* I believe the end of all things will be in "the rest of God." This is a secret thought of God—knowing when the end will end. God is so intelligent that He had His spoken Word written out. This was so every man would know some of His thoughts and some of His ways. God is keeping the end a "secret." This secret of time is still in the mind of God, and we don't know it *yet*. God has given us enough of His thoughts for us to be ready when the end comes. The book of Revelation gives us a view of what the end will look like, but it still doesn't tell us *when* we will see it. God has fixed it so that every nation will hear of His judgments and know that judgment is coming. One of the things God wants man to have is the same mind that Adam had in the beginning *before* he sinned. All Adam had in his mind was the thoughts or the righteousness of God. God had given him dominion over everything on earth, but not the things in the sky or heavens. I'm sure Adam named everything the same way God would have named it because Adam had a godly, righteous mind, and the language of God. Since Adam had a godly mind and the language of God, he would be able to make some of the same decisions as God. When we have the mind of God, we can call things that are not as though they were. We can call healing for the sick, deliverance to those who are despondent, and speak to the mountains and tell them to be removed.

We don't know the power of our words when we "echo" the thoughts of God in our speech. This is what this chapter is all about, using the right language. This language is the righteousness of God or the way He talks and does things. We must use the thoughts that God is thinking toward us. Not only will His thoughts give us peace, but they are words that will defend us when trouble comes. Godly speech can be used as our shield of faith and can be used as the "sword of the Spirit," which is the Word of God. Godly speech can be used as our helmet of salvation, and as a breastplate of righteousness, which guards our hearts. It can be used to shod our feet with the Gospel of the peace of Jesus Christ so we can walk by faith, not by sight. Whenever we receive the thoughts of God, and use it in our everyday speech, it can be used for our advantage and for our betterment.

Pentecost didn't "cost" us a penny. Pentecost was not just to receive the Holy Spirit, but to also receive the language of the Holy Spirit. Acts 2:4 says, "*And they were all filled with the Holy Ghost, and began to speak with other tongues, as the Spirit gave them utterance.*" The word "utterance" in the Greek is *rhema*, which means "things said" or "things spoken." It is the past tense of what God has already spoken. We commonly know it to be "inspiration" or "breath-in" for the languages spoken at Pentecost was the evidence that they had received the power that Jesus had promised them.

Nowhere in the Scriptures did anyone receive the Holy Ghost without speaking in an unknown tongue. On every occasion in Scripture, when it was received, there was always someone there to verify the unknown tongue. I know we often talk about speaking in an unknown tongue, but we don't often talk about the nations that were there. These nations were nations of Jews who spoke a different dialect; but when these nations heard those who were speaking in an unknown tongue, it was not "unknown" to the nations that were there. God was speaking through them with one tongue. But the nations, which spoke different languages or dialects, heard the same thing in their own language. They may have the same language being Jews. God was speaking again in "one" language, but they heard their language in the one language of God. Acts 2:7 says, *"And they were all amazed and marvelled, saying one to another, Behold, are not all these which speak Galilaeans? And how hear we every man in our own tongue, wherein we were born?"* They may not have understood one another, but they understood the language of God. God can speak "one" language from glory and, by the time it reaches the earth, all men with different languages will hear the same thing. Keep in mind that when God speaks His language, all men will hear the same thing.

Over time, man stopped listening to the thoughts and language of God. So, God must have thought of the Lamb that was slain before the foundation of the world. What language He used, I don't think anyone knows. Some say it was an angelic language; however, we still don't know what that language was. We will know it when we get to heaven because I do believe we all will speak the same language and have the same speech in glory.

This Lamb was again, the thought of God, that would save all men with different languages. This Lamb had a heavenly language; but when God sent this Lamb to the earth, this Lamb's language changed to a language of man or the language of the time. He healed with this language, gave sight to the blind and raised the dead. This Lamb was Jesus Christ. He chose twelve men to teach them the language of God, even with parables, in the language that they knew. They heard and saw what Jesus did with the language of God. They slept with Him, ate with Him, for about three years. But most of them learned to duplicate what he had spoken to them. So much so, when the people heard them talk, they said, "You must have been with Jesus, for you sound like Him." Acts 4:13 says, *"Now when they saw the boldness of Peter and John, and perceived that they were unlearned and ignorant men, they marvelled; and they took knowledge of them, that they had been with Jesus."*

Have you been with Jesus long enough that you sound like Him? Your language and speech will reveal that you have received, retained, and are able to repeat Him. When Jesus went to His own, He was rejected because He used the same language of man. But He was speaking a different "speech."

Now, the difference between "language" and "speech" is that language is what we learn by hearing words or thoughts. Language is a learning process that cannot be seen or heard. However, speech is the audible words that come out of our mouths from the language that's in our mind. We may not know a person's language until we hear that person's speech. So, our speech is a by-product of our language. Language is in our mind, but speech is in our mouths or tongue. Our language can stay in our mind, and no one will know what we are thinking. But if we want someone to know and hear what we are thinking, we'll put the words in our tongues to form our speech.

Jesus used the same language of men, but He used a different speech out of His mouth. His speech could calm a raging sea. Some enjoyed the benefits of this type of speech. But when Jesus said, "I and my Father are one," they didn't understand His speech at all. It was the same language, but a different speech. They said, "No one is equal to God," and they thought Jesus was blaspheming God. Blaspheming God always required death. When the same one who healed and delivered them rode into Jerusalem, they cried out, "Hosanna," which means, "Save us now." They were speaking the right language, but they didn't understand their speech. Jesus came to save them, but they didn't understand *how* He was going to save them.

When trouble arises, the blood of Jesus gives us the authority to use His name. A man named "Jones" cannot use the name "Lucas" because we are of a different DNA. Jesus' name only has one bloodline. Unsaved folks use the name, but they are unauthorized to use it. They may have a religion, but that doesn't mean they have a relationship by blood with Jesus. Those who are in Him are authorized to use His name. We have His DNA and are called the "sons of God."

So, the correct speech we should use when trouble arises is the name of Jesus, then the blood will be applied. We cannot use the blood without the name, and we cannot use the name without the blood. The name still works because the blood still works. We cannot borrow Jesus' name from someone who knows Jesus; we must know Him for ourselves. When we truly know Him for ourselves, we'll learn how to use the correct language and the correct speech by using the thoughts God is thinking toward us. Keep using the right language!

CHAPTER 9

NEVER STOP TALKING TO YOURSELF

In chapter three, we talked about "self-talk." Self-talk can cause worry and stress, and it can put our nerves on edge. It doesn't mean you're crazy; it's a normal process of thinking where most times we think the worse rather than the better. Our minds are treasure chests of information. It's like a computer where information is stored and is available whenever we need it. The Word of God is also a treasure chest of information, and it has a solution to every situation under the sun.

On May 6, 1967, I received the thought of God that He was thinking toward me. If you cannot self-talk about God filling you with His Holy Spirit, you are losing the best self-talk. If you are reading this book, you can thank God that you are still breathing. He has blessed your going out and your coming in. He has blessed you in the city and in the field. He has kept you from hurt, harm and danger.

One of the greatest elements of self-talk is remembrance. If God did something for us in the past, He could do it again in our present and in our future. We must keep reminding ourselves that if it weren't for the Lord on our side, who and where would we be? Each morning that we get from God, He is due thoughts of praise. Our thoughts ought to be as David said in Psalm 34:1 KJV, *"I will bless the LORD at all times: his praise shall continually be in my mouth."* David also said in Psalm 150:6, *"Let everything that hath breath praise the LORD. Praise ye the LORD."*

I believe the Psalms were written for the people of God to recite and sing in their service unto God. Now, a sinner can praise God, but I don't think their praises affect God like the praises of His people. David also wrote in Psalm 22:3, *"But Thou art holy, O Thou that inhabitest the praises of Israel."* Sinners may praise God, but will God inhabit their praises? We should freely use our mouths to offer praise to God. That's where our breath is. Our breath is where God looks to be praised and exalted. I have often said, "If a praise is not seen or heard, it's not a praise at all."

The purpose of God creating man, was for His pleasure, according to Revelation 4:11. God also created man with a mind and a mouth. So, whatever abides in the thinking of our mind would eventually come out of our mouths. God created man as a spiritual being. Whenever God creates another spirit, that spirit will always exist eternally, and reside in either hell or in heaven. If we use our thinking toward God, it will cause God's breath to breathe on us.

Sometimes, it's not our conscience talking to us. Our thinking can be "self-talk." Self-talk is when we are not trying to make a decision; we're simply talking within ourselves about things we have experienced, things that affect us in our present, and what we want to experience in the future. Self-talk can influence our conscience, our inner values and our moral principles as we evaluate situations in making decisions.

Self-talk is when we see a person's mouth moving and there is no sound coming out of their mouths. They are talking to themselves. No one can hear them outside of themselves and God. I am sure Satan listens, too. I believe Satan can read lips. Whatever we secretly promise God with our mouths, Satan tends to hinder, kill, steal and destroy. He will listen to our gossip, which can be evil words that come out of our mouth, and he can use gossip to influence our speech. It can be evil thoughts about our family, friends, neighbors, enemies and church.

When we have self-talk, it can be purposeful or random. Sometimes, our thoughts can influence how we feel, react, and even how we behave. Sometimes, self-talk can be thoughts you wish you would've said during a conversation or an argument. On the other hand, it could include the thoughts you wish you hadn't said. Self-talk can be an advantage or a disadvantage. We often don't know the difference between disadvantage and advantage thoughts without first having God in our thoughts.

Some believe Satan cannot read our minds, but I have had some real spiritual warfare in my mind. When Satan brings temptation to my mind, and I say in my mind, *Satan, The Lord rebuke you*, I can think a good thought and Satan has the tendency to counteract the thought in my mind. This reminds me of what Paul said in Romans 7:21 (KJV), *I find then a law, that, when I would do good, evil is present with me*. Some believe it's our human nature speaking to us. I found out Satan loves to work in our human nature. Satan cannot read our minds, but he certainly understands the thoughts coming out of our mouths. Satan will try his best to reel in our promises, anxieties and cares. We wonder why we continue to find ourselves dealing with the same troubles repeatedly.

Every promise we make to God will be accommodated by a problem. But every problem can be accommodated and answered by a verse from God's Word. Isaiah 59:19 (KJV) says, "*So shall they fear the name of the Lord from the west, and his glory from the rising of the sun. When the enemy shall come in like a flood, the Spirit of the LORD shall lift up a standard against him.*" If we don't have God's Spirit, there will not be any lifting against Satan's attack. The standards of God will accommodate every situation. For God to lift the standard, we must stand on God's standards, His promises, and His will.

We will always carry evil thoughts. It's in our human nature, and Satan loves to work in our human nature. If Satan cannot read our minds, he certainly can read our lips. It is where the "old man" exists to remind us of how we used to act and think, which was out of order with God's standards. Our old nature should be dead in our thinking. Isaiah 26:3 (KJV) says, *"Thou wilt keep him in perfect peace, whose mind (thinking) is stayed on thee:"* *"To stay"* means God has set up residence in our mind because He trusts us. He will keep our mind in perfect peace. This is the same peace that's in Jeremiah 29:11.

The word "peace" in the Hebrew is *shalom*. It doesn't just mean peace; it also means rest, completeness and wholeness. In self-talk, we need all the meanings. This is the shalom that God is thinking toward us. It is important to bring God into the conversation in our minds. We can do this by putting a Scripture or two there from the Bible that are fitting for the situation at hand. We can repeat God's Word in our self-talk until we can speak it through our mouths and our deeds. If we repetitiously think about praise, praise will come out of our mouths. It will be in our hands and feet. Everything we say or do first travels through our mind, or our thinking, as a thought.

We can self-talk our way into a lot of trouble, but we must let God talk us out of trouble. This is why we must do as David said, "to meditate" on God's Word, day and night. This is why I'm encouraging you to keep talking to yourself about God and talking to God. David said in Psalm 19:14 (KJV), *"Let the words of my mouth, and the meditation of my heart, be acceptable in thy sight, O LORD, my strength and my redeemer."* God's Word is our redeemer and our strength. It will help us stay out of trouble when our mind is stayed on Him. Solomon said, *"There is a time to be silent and a time to speak, and a time to keep our mouth shut."* But what has happened is that we don't think enough about what God says before we speak. We should evaluate our thoughts by asking ourselves the question, "Will my thought hurt or help in this situation?" "Is this what God would want me to say?" When we have self-talk about what God has done, it will cause us to praise God and think ourselves happy. I believe God wants us to think about Him in every situation. I hope you never stop talking to yourself about God or stop talking directly to God. Allow God's Word to be the final resolve of every decision in your life.

CHAPTER 10
BE CAREFUL USING, "AMEN!"

I want to close this book with one of the most important words we use in church or in response to what someone says. That word is, "Amen." Whenever we use the word "Amen," we are agreeing with what is said or what has been done. Whatever a person says or does, we should understand or know for ourselves whether it is worthy of an, *"Amen."* Before we co-sign it, we should be sure that it is information that can be verified in the Word of God.

If we do not know, nor understand what we are saying, "Amen" to, we should hold up on our agreeance until we get better knowledge of what the speaker has said and what they mean. Placing "Amen" on what someone says will put us in a place where we become one with them—whether right or wrong.

I remember a time in church when a guest minister was prophesying to the congregation. I heard a person next to me say, "Amen" to the prophesy. But when we left the sanctuary, they asked me, "What did he mean when he said that?" My reply to them was, "I heard you say, "Amen" to what he said, and I thought you understood!" They went on to say, "I felt that he is a good prophet, so I just believed that he was speaking the truth." I said to this person what my dad often said to me: "He's just a man like you, and we all can be wrong." My dad also told me, "If Satan can lie in heaven, then he has no problem telling a lie in church." It is concerning to me how quickly people will co-sign something by saying, "Amen" to it, even when they have no real understanding of what they are co-signing.

In this scenario, I'm not saying that the person who was prophesying told a lie. But Satan can and will use anybody, including pastors, teachers, deacons, saints and friends to say something that's not true. Oftentimes, what people say comes from their own perceptions. Let's just call a spade a spade. If it is a lie, it's a lie. Truth is one of the elements of life that can be twisted so that anytime anything is mixed with it, it loses its significance. It still may sound good; however, whatever sounds good may not be truly founded in truth. Every good-looking thing may not be a God thing!

I was in a service where a person was preparing to prophesy. They said, "Stand if you have a financial problem." I thought about standing, and I'm sure most of the people in the sanctuary could have stood up, too. The prophet said to one brother, "Money cometh!" and the young man said,

"Amen." I asked the brother a few weeks later, "Did the money come yet?" He said, "I wish it was true because I haven't received anything yet."

My former mentor, Elder Tommy Wood, used to say, "Whatever sounds good may not be sound doctrine." This is why we all should be careful when using the word, "Amen." It puts us in agreement with something that may not be true.

"Amen" is a statement by itself. We can put a period behind each "Amen." "Amen" is a doxology (ending) by itself every time we say it. It's a mental and spiritual decision that will cause us to live a lie or obligate us to perform a request made by someone else. There is something unique about the word, "Amen." The Old Testament was written in Hebrew, and the New Testament was written in Greek. Both testaments spell the word "amen" with the same letters and they carry the same connotation. Connotation means the same idea or feeling that a word invokes. In the Hebrew, the word "amen" means "fixed or firm." In Judaism, they believe that whatever God says is already fixed or done. Once again, it is doxology by itself.

In Arabic, "Amen" means to be "devoted to" or "Whatever Allah says, I will do." As Christians, we understand that the New Testament is written from the Greek language and translated into English. "Amen" means, "it is so" or "Whatever Jesus says, I agree with." So, the word, "Amen" has the same connotation among all these religions. It gives the sense of, "I will agree with whatever God says, does, or even what He desires to do." When we say, "Amen" to God, even to Jesus Christ, it's like signing our name on a contract or a covenant with God. He will keep His word; He looks for us to keep ours. The only way we can keep our part is to know and do His part, or what He says.

As Christians, it behooves us to understand what Jesus said and why He said what He said. Jesus spoke in parables to make sense to His listeners. He wanted them to understand heavenly principles. I am sure we all have read what He said at some point in our life. But to be honest, sometimes it's not easy to say or act out the, "Amen" to what He said. It's not easy to say, "Amen" to God when we lose a loved one. It's not easy to say, "Amen" when lose our homes, cars and money. It's not easy to say, "Amen" to the pains and tragedies of life. It's not easy to say, "Amen" unless we understand God's sovereignty. Whatever He says or does, we can put an, "Amen" on it.

There is a difference between translation and transliteration. Transliteration is when a word does not lose its meaning from one language to another. Translation is when the word is written from one language into another. Most times, the meaning may vary in its definition or application. We have a lot of Bibles that have been translated from one language into another. Some have lost some real meaning though.

The Hebrew word in Isaiah 7:14 is "almah," and its inherent meaning is "young woman." Whereas, in the King James Version of the Bible, that same verse says, *"Behold a virgin shall conceive and bear a son."* A 'young girl' doesn't automatically mean 'a virgin.' Thus, the translation can be deceiving. Deception can be a trick of Satan, regardless of who has translated it. It can, in many cases, lose its real or contextual meaning.

There is a principle in hermeneutics called "the principle of first mention." When a word is first mentioned, it must have the same continuity as when it was first mentioned. A virgin is a virgin each time it's mentioned. It was a virgin who gave birth to the Son of God, and not just a "young girl." So, in Scripture, an, "Amen" is an "Amen" each time it is mentioned. I often use the King James Version of the Bible because it gives me the closest apostolic view of the Bible, or the oneness of God. Therefore, whatever Bible translation you use to gain the truth of God, pray before you read any alternative translation of the Bible before you say, "Amen" to it. The Holy Spirit will help you understand it or even let you know whether it's true.

Before you put your, "Amen" on an interpretation that sounds good, ask yourself, "Is it sound doctrine?" A doctrine of Scripture must be mentioned at least three times with the same connotation or context. If we examine "baptism" with all languages, it should mean the same thing. In some religious persuasions, baptism is a total emersion into water. In other religions, it means the sprinkling of water on the head of the person. What's so amazing is that different religions can read from the same source yet still come up with very different understandings.

Baptism is mentioned three or more times in Acts. The book of Acts chronicles the beginning of the Church. Thus, it is particularly important that it has continuity. Baptism in the name of the Father, Son and Holy Spirit is only mentioned once, and we never read where this type of baptism was done again. Jesus said in Matthew 18:16, "*Out of the mouths of two or three, let every word be "established."* It is important to say, "Amen" to a doctrine that is well established by Scripture. There are times the Scriptures can be difficult to agree with. Not too many can say, "Amen" to *"Love your enemies and do good to them that despitefully use you."* So, the question is, what do we say when it's hard to say, "Amen"? It's hard to agree with God when there are different opinions. What usually comes out of our mouths is not agreement, but the question of, "Why, Lord?" or "Why me?" We tend to thank God or agree with Him for the good times and good things; but then we question Him when bad things happen to us.

We must learn a lesson from Job. In Job 1:21-22 (KJV), God places Job in a fight that Job didn't start; however, God had written Job's resume. God said Job was a perfect and upright man, one who feared God and eschewed evil. After he had lost everything, Job said, *"Naked came I out of my mother's womb, and naked shall I return thither:* (he was from "dust" and to dust" he would return) *the Lord gave, and the Lord hath taken away; blessed be the name of the Lord.* Job 1:22 says, *"In all this Job sinned not, nor charged God foolishly."* Job didn't have the Adam and Eve syndrome where he started blaming others. Job accepted his condition. In his condition, he must have said, "Amen." This thought is found in Job 14:14: *"If a man die, shall he live again? All the days of my appointed time will I wait, until my change comes."*

It's okay to question God. I am sure we all have a lot of questions, but we must be ready to receive His answers and be ready to agree with them. We ought to know that sometimes (and life is full of sometimes), God's answers do not always agree with us. If we do not understand God's sovereignty, we will charge God foolishly. Sometimes, we self-impose challenging times on ourselves. Then, we ask, "Why me, Lord?" We should never blame God for all our misfortunes, faults and failures. When we are not following the thoughts of God, it's easy for us to find ourselves saying, "Amen" to carnal things or to something Satan has offered us to tempt us. The lesson is to be careful when we say, "Amen" and to whom we're saying it. We may be signing a contract with Satan or even saying, "Amen" to our own selfish desires. This is pride, which always leads to destruction.

It also behooves us to listen to what the preacher or teacher is saying. However, we must also check and find out whether what they're saying is scripturally within the proper context. We shouldn't be so quick to say, "Amen" to everything we hear. How many of us have sat in church and said, "Amen" to something we don't understand? We say, "Amen" because a certain person is speaking or because they seem like they're making a lot of sense. However, making a lot of sense may not be making a lot of truth, which produces faith. Faith comes by hearing; but lies also come by hearing.

I am praying that the saints will listen more than they shout. People are having a good time in church, but they leave church without knowing what their "Amen" meant. We are in a time where we listen more to music than the message in the music. We must have an attentive ear to hear. God has given us a special set of ears called the Holy Ghost. These "ears" are for us to hear what the Spirit is saying to the Church. We will leave our churches the same way we came if we don't listen. I hear a lot of preachers preaching just to make folks shout. But if our shout doesn't have an,

"Amen" in it, we are only doing physical exercise. Be careful when you say, "Amen." It's an agreement that connects us to a thought. Our listening will affect our thoughts. Hearing is one thing, but listening is another.

Every sermon is not of God. Some messages may be the thought of God, but the delivery may be a speaker's own thoughts. I am sure, when Jesus said, "*Verily, verily I say unto you…*," it was for us to pay attention to what He was about to say. When Jesus said these words, He always followed them with the truth. May I say unto you, Verily, verily I say unto you, always have an ear to listen to the thoughts that God is thinking toward you. Get all you can, and *can* all you get, especially to what is written. If you don't think you need it now, you will need it eventually.

Be careful when you say, "Yes" or "Amen" to God. He will hold our feet to the fire, and we will feel like Jeremiah, like fire shut up in our bones. Whatever God asks us to do will be His righteous thoughts toward us. If God asks us to do anything for Him, He will be right there with us. Usually, when God asks something of us, He knows we already have it in the sense that He has already provided it. He wants it to be for His glory, not ours. There are times when God will ask us to do something we have never done before, and we feel it's outside of our ability. We cannot find it in our mind or hands to do it. But if we put our, "Amen" on it, it gives God the opportunity to fulfill His ability in us.

When God saved us, He gave us His Holy Spirit. When God gave us His Spirit, the Spirit had all the gifts in it. However, we did not know which gift God wanted to use in us. There are three types of gifts in the Spirit. The number one gift is our primary gift, the one you know God is using you in. Then, there is what I call the number two or secondary gift, the gift that God often uses in us as needed in a situation to which we must react. We may have the word of knowledge as a primary gift, but God may have you lay hands on the sick to be healed. He may have you speak a message like a preacher to someone in need of a word from God. But the third type of gift is what I call a "surprise gift." That's when we can be totally "surprised" that God used us in a way that was baffling and unexpected. We shouldn't be surprised, simply because we have God's Spirit with all the gifts in it. All we must do is put an, "Amen" on the gifts.

The Apostle Paul (Saul, before his conversion) was intelligent; yet, with all his intelligence, he wasn't spiritual. He tried to destroy the church, even the concept of grace. He used the law to destroy the saints. On his way to persecute the Church, God stepped into his journey with His glory, a light that could not be ignored. Saul was kicking in the wrong direction and misguided with the wrong thought. So, Jesus pricked Saul spiritually with the rod of correction. This "prick" changed Saul's life. He was convicted, convinced and converted to Christianity. His name was changed to Paul and now, as Paul, he placed his, "Amen" on this experience.

Now faith is our, "Amen" to whatever God's thoughts are toward us. Now we can put our "Amen" on the truth rather than a lie. Again, be careful who and what you put your "Amen" on. Keep your "Amen" on God. I pray that this book has encouraged you to study and find God's thoughts that are toward you. May the Lord bless you and keep you. May the Lord cause His Face to shine upon you and be gracious unto you. May the Lord lift His countenance upon you and give you peace. Be blessed, in Jesus' name. Selah.

CIVIC RESOLUTION HONORING DISTRICT ELDER JOHN M. LUCAS

WHEREAS, We, the Wayne County Commission, is proud to honor and celebrate the retirement of DISTRICT ELDER JOHN M. LUCAS on this day, July 14, 2024; and

WHEREAS, ELDER LUCAS was called to the ministry over forty years ago under the leadership of the late Tommy Wood at Bethel Church of the Apostolic Faith, and has since faithfully served in numerous capacities including Assistant Pastor, Youth Pastor, Pastor of Christian Education, Catechism Instructor, and a member of the official board; and

WHEREAS, ELDER LUCAS has been an active member of the Northern District Council of the Pentecostal Assemblies of the World, having served on the Election and Grievance Committee, Planning Committee, and as a Lay Director, embodying the spirit of servant leadership as Christ commanded; and

WHEREAS, ELDER LUCAS demonstrated his prowess and dedication to our country as a U.S. Army Sergeant/SP5, receiving the Purple Heart, Combat Medical Badge, Distinguished Bronze Star, Medal with "V" (for valor), Vietnam Service Medal, National Defense Service Medal, Vietnam Campaign Medal, Marksman Badge, and Good Conduct Medal-First Award; and

WHEREAS, ELDER LUCAS after a distinguished 30+ year career at General Dynamics Land Systems, he retired to dedicate himself fully to pastoring Bethel Church of the Apostolic Faith, and was appointed Honorary Bishop in 2019 by Apostle James Kellem, Presiding Prelate of the Dominion Covenant Fellowship of Churches International; and

WHEREAS, ELDER LUCAS has continuously given back to his community by operating a food bank both out of his home and the church, serving as a mentor and father figure to males from single-parent homes, and tirelessly working to feed the flock of GOD, as he believes his mandate from the LORD to be; and

WHEREAS, ELDER LUCAS, together with his former wife (Lady Dorothy Lucas) raised three children before she passed in 2012. After which, he married (Lady Louanne Lucas) and has been a steadfast example of a Godly husband and father; and

WHEREAS, ELDER LUCAS, has prepared the saints for ministry, equipping and birthing Preachers, Teachers,

Evangelists, Missionaries, and Pastors, ensuring the legacy of his church and the continuation of its divine mission;

NOW, THEREFORE BE IT RESOLVED, That the Wayne County Commission honor DISTRICT ELDER JOHN M. LUCAS for his unwavering dedication and service. As he steps into retirement, we recognize that his journey is not the end but a transition into a season of reaping the fruits of his labor, as Galatians 6:9 (KJV) reminds us, *"And let us not be weary in well doing: for in due season we shall reap, if we faint not."* Let this resolution be laid across the pages of the Journal of the Wayne County Commission in perpetuity.

JONATHAN C. KINLOCH
Wayne County Commission, District 2

ABOUT THE AUTHOR

While many chase after accolades, awards and affirmations, his sole purpose is to edify and exhort the people of God and usher them into their destiny assignment. With over 40 years of ministerial and leadership experience, Pastor Emeritus John M. Lucas is intentional about equipping preachers, teachers, evangelists, missionaries and pastors for success in ministry. As a legacy builder, change agent and mentor to many, he works tirelessly to impact his community inside and outside the four walls of the church. Unlike many who are content with giving someone a fish, he teaches others how to fish so they can be a kingdom resource to others.

Having served in many capacities of his local church, Pastor Lucas has had the honor of being the assistant pastor, youth pastor, pastor of Christian education, catechism instructor and a member of the official church board. As an active member of the Northern District Council of the Pentecostal Assemblies of the World (PAW), he also served on the Election and Grievance Committee, Planning

Committee and as a Lay Director. Pastor Lucas also served our country as a U.S. Army Sergeant/SP5 where he was the recipient of the Purple Heart, Combat Medical Badge, Distinguished Bronze Star, Medal with "V" (for valor), Vietnam Service Medal, National Defense Service Medal, Vietnam Campaign Medal, Marksman Badge, and Good Conduct Medal-First Award. Whether he's been on the battlefield for the country or the Lord, his tenacity, courage and boldness are left to be desired by many.

In his debut book, *The Advantages & Disadvantages of Thoughts*, Pastor Lucas challenges readers to take an intimate look at their own thought patterns and how they align, or misalign, with their goals and vision. Encouraging readers to be occupied with the Word and cultivating the mind of Christ, Lucas reminds readers to focus on what God has done, what He is doing, and what He will do in the future. This book serves as a guide for the people of God to stand on the promises of God, decipher God's permissive will vs. His perfect will for their lives and train their thoughts to line up with the Word.

After working more than 30 years for General Dynamics Land Systems, fifteen of which he worked as a tool engineer, Pastor Lucas retired to pastor Bethel Church of the Apostolic Faith fulltime, where he serves today. Having operated a food bank both out of his home and the church, he has served as a mentor and coach to males of all ages. Pastor Lucas resides in a suburb of Detroit with his loving wife, Evangelist LouAnne Lucas and is the father of three children.